Surviving One-L: Navigating the First Year of Law School with Confidence

Welcome to the exhilarating and challenging world of law school! As you embark on your journey into the legal profession, you are about to experience the transformative and intellectually stimulating first year, commonly known as "One-L." This period is a critical foundation for your legal education and sets the stage for your future career as a lawyer.

In "Surviving One-L: Navigating the First Year of Law School with Confidence," we are committed to being your trusted guide and companion throughout this transformative year. We understand that the journey can be daunting and overwhelming, but we firmly believe that with the right mindset, support, and strategies, you can excel and thrive.

This comprehensive guide is designed to provide you with the essential tools, insights, and wisdom to navigate the complexities of law school successfully. Whether you are a recent college graduate, a career changer, or someone pursuing a lifelong passion for the law, this book is tailored to meet your needs and empower you to make the most of your One-L experience.

In these pages, you will find practical advice on a wide range of topics, including:

1. Preparing for Law School: We kick off by helping you set the stage for your law school journey. From understanding the application process and selecting the right law school to tips on acing the LSAT, we ensure you start on the right foot.

2. Surviving the First Semester: The first semester of One-L is known for its intensity and rigor. We guide you through core subjects, the Socratic method, and the art of legal reasoning, ensuring you build a strong academic foundation.

3. Legal Research and Writing: Proficiency in legal research and writing is the backbone of your legal education. We provide valuable insights into legal research techniques and mastering the art of persuasive legal writing.

4. Balancing Academic and Personal Life: Maintaining a healthy work-life balance is crucial for your well-being and academic success. We share strategies for managing stress, staying organized, and finding time for personal growth and self-care.

5. Building Professional Connections: Networking is an essential aspect of your legal journey. We offer tips on building meaningful connections with professors, peers, and legal professionals.

6. Preparing for Exams: Finals season can be nerve-wracking, but with our proven study strategies and exam preparation techniques, you can approach exams with confidence and competence.

7. Navigating Challenges: The road to becoming a lawyer may have its share of challenges. From imposter syndrome to dealing with setbacks, we provide support and motivation to overcome obstacles.

"Surviving One-L" is not just a guidebook; it is a companion that will empower you to embrace your legal education with confidence and determination. We are excited to be part of your journey as you discover the fascinating world of law and set the stage for a successful and fulfilling career. Let us embark on this transformative journey together and embrace the possibilities that One-L offers.

I. Introduction

- Welcome to the world of law school
- The significance of the first year: One-L
- The journey to mastering the art of law practice

II. Preparing for Law School

- The law school application process
- Selecting the right law school
- Acing the LSAT: Tips and strategies
- Financial planning and scholarships

III. Surviving the First Semester

- Embracing the Socratic method and legal reasoning
- Understanding core subjects: Contracts, Torts, and Criminal Law
- Case briefing and legal analysis
- Time management and study strategies

IV. Legal Research and Writing

- Mastering legal research techniques
- The art of persuasive legal writing
- Writing case briefs and memos
- Effective use of legal citations

V. Balancing Academic and Personal Life

- Managing stress and avoiding burnout
- Time management and organization skills

- Finding a support network and seeking help when needed
- Prioritizing self-care and well-being

VI. Building Professional Connections

- The importance of networking in the legal profession
- Building relationships with professors and peers
- Engaging with legal professionals and alumni
- Leveraging social media for professional development

VII. Preparing for Exams

- Strategies for effective exam preparation
- Outlining and review techniques
- Practice exams and mock sessions
- Tips for handling exam day stress

VIII. Navigating Challenges

- Dealing with imposter syndrome and self-doubt
- Coping with setbacks and failures
- Seeking academic and emotional support
- Fostering resilience and growth mindset

IX. Legal Ethics and Professionalism

- Understanding the importance of legal ethics
- Professional responsibility in law school and beyond
- Ethics in legal research and writing
- Upholding integrity in legal practice

X. Looking Ahead: Preparing for the Next Steps

- Exploring legal internships and externships
- Mapping out your legal career path
- Exploring specialty areas of law
- Setting long-term goals for your legal journey

XI. Conclusion

- Reflecting on your One-L journey
- Embracing the challenges and rewards of law school
- Continuing the pursuit of mastering the art of law practice
- Parting words of encouragement and motivation

Welcome to the world of law school

Thank you! Law school is an exciting and challenging journey that offers a unique opportunity to delve into the intricacies of the legal system, develop critical thinking skills, and prepare for a rewarding career in the legal profession. As you embark on this new chapter, you'll have the chance to explore various areas of law, engage in rigorous legal research and analysis, and participate in thought-provoking class discussions.

Throughout law school, you'll be exposed to a diverse range of legal subjects, from constitutional law and contracts to criminal law and property law. The classroom experience will be complemented by opportunities for hands-on learning, such as moot court competitions, legal clinics, and internships, where you can apply your knowledge in real-world settings.

Law school is not just about academics; it's also about personal growth and building professional connections. You'll have the chance to interact with faculty members, fellow students, and legal professionals, creating a network that can be invaluable throughout your career.

While law school can be demanding, it is also a time of self-discovery and intellectual exploration. Embrace the challenges, stay curious, and be open to new perspectives. Remember that each step in this journey is a building block towards becoming a skilled and compassionate legal advocate.

As you navigate through law school, remember that there is no one-size-fits-all approach to success. Find your own balance between academics, extracurricular activities, and self-care. Take advantage of the resources and support available to you, and don't hesitate to seek guidance from professors and mentors.

Welcome to the world of law school! Embrace the opportunities it offers, stay focused on your goals, and let the journey of legal education shape you into a dedicated and knowledgeable legal professional. Best of luck on this exciting path!

The significance of the first year: One-L

The first year of law school, often referred to as "One-L," holds immense significance in a law student's academic and professional journey. It is a crucial foundational year that sets the tone for the rest of your legal education and career. Here are some reasons why the first year is so important:

1. Introduction to Legal Concepts: During the first year, you will be introduced to fundamental legal concepts and principles. Courses like Contracts, Torts, Civil Procedure, and Criminal Law will provide the building blocks of legal analysis and reasoning.

2. Legal Research and Writing Skills: Law school's first year emphasizes legal research and writing, essential skills for any lawyer. You'll learn how to research case law, statutes, and legal doctrines, as well as how to construct persuasive legal arguments.

3. Grading and Class Rank: The first-year grades often have a significant impact on your class rank, which can influence future job opportunities and clerkship applications.

4. Joining Law Reviews and Journals: Many prestigious law reviews and journals select their members based on first-year academic performance and writing competitions.

5. Bar Exam Preparation: The material covered in the first year is foundational for the bar exam. Strong performance in these courses will aid in bar exam preparation down the line.

6. Building Relationships: The first year is an excellent

time to build relationships with professors, classmates, and legal professionals. Networking and mentorship can be invaluable throughout your legal career.

7. Time Management and Discipline: Law school can be demanding, and the first year teaches you valuable time management and discipline skills to balance academic work and extracurricular activities.

8. Exposure to Different Areas of Law: By taking core courses in various areas of law, you'll gain exposure to different legal specialties and can make more informed decisions about your future career path.

9. Legal Culture and Terminology: The first year immerses you in the legal culture and introduces you to the unique terminology and practices of the legal profession.

10. Setting a Strong Foundation: Mastering the material in the first year sets a strong foundation for more advanced legal studies and helps you approach legal issues with analytical precision.

While the first year can be challenging, it is also an exciting time of growth and intellectual exploration. Embrace the experience, seek support when needed, and remember that your hard work and dedication during this crucial year will lay the groundwork for a successful legal career.

The journey to mastering the art of law practice

The journey to mastering the art of law practice is a dynamic and continuous process that requires dedication, perseverance, and a commitment to lifelong learning. It involves a series of steps and experiences that shape legal professionals into skilled advocates and counselors. Here is an overview of the key stages in the journey to mastering the art of law practice:

1. Legal Education: The journey begins with obtaining a law degree from an accredited law school. Legal education lays the foundation for understanding the principles of law, legal analysis, research, and writing.

2. Bar Examination and Licensing: After completing law school, aspiring lawyers must pass the bar examination in their jurisdiction to obtain a license to practice law. This step ensures that lawyers meet the necessary standards of competency and ethics.

3. Early Career Experience: New attorneys gain valuable experience and practical skills by working in law firms, government agencies, or legal clinics. Early career experiences provide exposure to various areas of law and real-world legal challenges.

4. Mentoring and Guidance: Throughout their careers, legal professionals benefit from mentorship and guidance from experienced lawyers. Mentors offer valuable insights, support, and feedback to help young attorneys develop their skills and navigate the legal profession.

5. Specialization and Expertise: As legal professionals gain experience, they may choose to specialize in specific areas of law, such as litigation, corporate law, intellectual property, or family law. Specialization allows attorneys to develop deep expertise in their chosen field.

6. Continuing Legal Education: Legal practitioners engage in continuing legal education (CLE) to stay abreast of changes in the law, emerging legal trends, and best practices. CLE programs enhance skills, broaden knowledge, and promote professional growth.

7. Building a Client Base: Mastering the art of law practice involves effectively attracting and retaining clients. Building a strong client base requires exceptional legal skills, reputation, and a focus on delivering exceptional client service.

8. Advocacy and Communication: Effective communication and advocacy skills are fundamental to mastering the art of law practice. Legal professionals must be adept at presenting arguments, negotiating, and persuasively advocating for their clients' interests.

9. Ethical Practice: Ethical conduct is integral to the practice of law. Mastering the art of law involves upholding the highest ethical standards, maintaining client confidentiality, and adhering to professional rules and responsibilities.

10. Leadership and Mentorship: As legal professionals gain experience, they may assume leadership roles within their firms, organizations, or legal communities. They may also serve as mentors to guide and inspire the next generation of lawyers.

11. Adapting to Change: The legal profession is constantly evolving, and mastering the art of law practice involves embracing technological advancements, new legal trends, and changes in the legal landscape.

12. Contributing to the Legal Community: Mastering the

art of law practice is not only about personal success but also about contributing to the legal community and society at large. Legal professionals can use their skills to advocate for social justice, access to justice, and the public good.

The journey to mastering the art of law practice is a lifelong endeavor characterized by continuous growth, professional development, and a commitment to excellence. It is a rewarding path that empowers legal professionals to make a positive impact on the lives of their clients and communities while upholding the principles of justice and the rule of law.

Preparing for Law School

Preparing for law school is an essential step in setting a solid foundation for a successful legal education and career. Here are some key steps to help you prepare for law school:

1. Research Law Schools: Research different law schools to find the ones that align with your academic and career goals. Consider factors such as location, faculty, programs, and areas of specialization.
2. Take Relevant Courses: While in college or before starting law school, consider taking courses related to law, such as political science, history, philosophy, or business law. These courses can provide a basic understanding of legal principles.
3. Develop Strong Writing Skills: Legal writing is a fundamental aspect of law school. Focus on developing strong writing skills, including clear and concise expression of ideas and critical analysis.
4. Improve Reading Comprehension: Law school involves a significant amount of reading, including cases, statutes, and legal opinions. Practice reading complex texts and enhance your reading comprehension skills.
5. Time Management: Law school can be demanding, so practice effective time management to balance academic work, extracurricular activities, and personal life.
6. Enhance Critical Thinking: Law school emphasizes critical thinking and analytical reasoning. Engage in activities that promote critical thinking, such as debating, mock trials, or participating in legal-related

discussions.

7. Familiarize Yourself with Legal Concepts: Read introductory law books or legal articles to familiarize yourself with basic legal concepts and terminologies.

8. Participate in Internships or Volunteering: Gain practical experience by interning at law firms, legal clinics, or government agencies. Volunteering in community organizations can also provide valuable insights into legal issues.

9. Practice Public Speaking: Public speaking is crucial for legal practice. Participate in public speaking events or join debate clubs to build confidence in expressing ideas verbally.

10. Attend Pre-Law Programs: Consider enrolling in pre-law programs or workshops that offer an overview of law school expectations and academic preparation.

11. Focus on Research Skills: Law school requires strong research skills. Practice legal research using legal databases and resources to familiarize yourself with the process.

12. Maintain a Strong GPA: Law schools often consider undergraduate GPA during the admissions process. Strive to maintain a strong academic record.

13. Seek Advice from Law Students or Lawyers: Connect with current law students or legal professionals to seek advice and insights into law school life and the legal profession.

Remember that law school is a challenging but rewarding experience. Preparing beforehand can help you feel more confident and ready to tackle the academic rigors of law school. Embrace the journey, stay focused on your goals, and enjoy the process of becoming a legal professional. Good luck on your journey to law school!

The law school application process

The law school application process is a crucial step in pursuing a legal education and preparing for a career in law. Here's an overview of the typical law school application process:

1. Research Law Schools: Start by researching different law schools to find the ones that align with your interests, career goals, and academic achievements. Consider factors such as location, reputation, areas of specialization, and bar passage rates.
2. Prepare for the LSAT: The Law School Admission Test (LSAT) is a standardized test that most law schools require for admission. Prepare for the LSAT by taking practice exams, attending review courses, and familiarizing yourself with the test format and question types.
3. Request Letters of Recommendation: Reach out to professors, employers, or mentors who know you well and can provide strong letters of recommendation. Choose individuals who can speak to your academic abilities, work ethic, and character.
4. Write a Personal Statement: Craft a compelling personal statement that highlights your motivations for pursuing a legal education, your experiences, and your aspirations in the legal field. Tailor your statement to each law school you apply to.
5. Gather Transcripts and Academic Records: Obtain official transcripts from all undergraduate institutions you attended. Law schools typically require these transcripts as part of the application.

6. Complete the Application: Complete the law school application form for each school you wish to apply to. Pay attention to specific application requirements, deadlines, and any additional materials needed, such as a resume or diversity statement.

7. Submit LSAT Scores: Request that your LSAT scores be sent directly to the law schools you are applying to. Most law schools accept LSAT scores from the past five years.

8. Pay Application Fees: Many law schools require an application fee. Pay the required fee for each school you apply to, or inquire about fee waivers if applicable.

9. Apply Early: Consider applying early in the admissions cycle to increase your chances of acceptance and potentially secure scholarships or financial aid.

10. Attend Interviews (if required): Some law schools conduct interviews as part of the admissions process. If invited for an interview, prepare thoroughly and showcase your passion for law and your fit for the school.

11. Await Admission Decisions: After submitting your applications, patiently await admission decisions from the law schools. Admissions decisions are typically communicated via email or postal mail.

12. Compare Offers and Make a Decision: Once you receive acceptance letters, carefully consider the offers, scholarship opportunities, and program offerings at each law school before making a final decision.

It is essential to be organized, diligent, and attentive to deadlines throughout the application process. Applying to law school is a competitive and rigorous process, but with proper preparation and a compelling application, you can increase your chances of gaining admission to the law school of your choice. Good luck in your law school journey!

Selecting the right law school

Selecting the right law school is a critical decision that can significantly impact your legal education and future career. Here are some factors to consider when choosing the right law school for you:

1. Location: Consider the location of the law school and whether you prefer to study in a specific city, state, or region. Location can affect your access to legal job markets and networking opportunities.
2. Reputation and Ranking: Review the law school's reputation and ranking in national and regional law school rankings. While rankings should not be the sole determinant, they can offer insights into the school's academic quality and recognition.
3. Areas of Specialization: Evaluate the law school's areas of specialization and programs. If you have a specific legal interest or career goal, choose a school that offers strong programs in those areas.
4. Bar Passage Rates: Check the law school's bar passage rates to determine how well graduates perform on the bar exam. High bar passage rates can indicate the effectiveness of the school's bar preparation programs.
5. Faculty and Resources: Look into the qualifications and expertise of the law school's faculty. Consider whether the school offers resources such as legal clinics, internships, or opportunities for hands-on learning.
6. Class Size and Student-to-Faculty Ratio: Consider the size of the law school's student body and the student-to-faculty ratio. Smaller class sizes may offer more

personalized attention and interaction with professors.

7. Career Services and Alumni Network: Research the law school's career services office and the strength of its alumni network. A robust career services department can help with job placements and networking opportunities.

8. Cost and Financial Aid: Evaluate the cost of tuition, fees, and living expenses. Research scholarship opportunities, grants, and financial aid packages offered by the law school.

9. Campus Culture and Environment: Visit the law school if possible or attend virtual events to get a sense of the campus culture, student life, and overall environment.

10. Bar Admission Requirements: If you plan to practice law in a specific jurisdiction, ensure that the law school's program meets the bar admission requirements of that jurisdiction.

11. Diversity and Inclusion: Consider the law school's commitment to diversity and inclusion. Look for a school that fosters a welcoming and inclusive environment.

12. Alumni Success and Employment Rates: Research the employment outcomes and success of the law school's alumni. Look for high employment rates and successful careers in various legal fields.

Remember that the right law school for you may differ from someone else's, and what matters most is finding a school that aligns with your academic goals, career aspirations, and personal preferences. Take the time to research and visit schools, talk to current students and alumni, and carefully weigh your options before making your final decision.

Acing the LSAT: Tips and strategies

Acing the Law School Admission Test (LSAT) is a crucial step in the law school application process. The LSAT is designed to assess your critical thinking, analytical reasoning, logical reasoning, and reading comprehension skills. Here are some tips and strategies to help you excel on the LSAT:

1. Start Early: Begin your LSAT preparation well in advance. Give yourself sufficient time to study and familiarize yourself with the test format and question types.
2. Understand the Test Format: Familiarize yourself with the structure and sections of the LSAT. The test consists of multiple-choice questions and an unscored writing sample.
3. Take Practice Tests: Practice tests are essential for LSAT preparation. Take several full-length practice tests under timed conditions to simulate the actual test environment.
4. Analyze Practice Tests: Review your performance on practice tests to identify areas of strength and weakness. Focus on improving weak areas through targeted study.
5. Study with Official LSAT Prep Materials: Use official LSAT preparation materials provided by the Law School Admission Council (LSAC). These materials are the most accurate representation of the test.
6. Work on Logical Reasoning: Logical reasoning questions make up a significant portion of the LSAT. Practice identifying the premises, conclusions, and logical

relationships in arguments.

7. Master Analytical Reasoning (Logic Games): Logic games can be challenging, but with practice, you can improve your skills. Learn different game types and practice setting up diagrams and making inferences.

8. Improve Reading Comprehension: Read challenging articles and passages to enhance your reading comprehension skills. Practice summarizing main ideas and identifying the author's tone and perspective.

9. Time Management: The LSAT is a timed test, so practice managing your time effectively. Learn to allocate time wisely to complete each section within the allotted time.

10. Utilize LSAT Prep Courses: Consider enrolling in LSAT prep courses, either in-person or online, to receive structured instruction, guidance, and access to additional resources.

11. Simulate Test Conditions: When taking practice tests, mimic the actual testing conditions as closely as possible. Use a quiet environment and adhere to the timing restrictions.

12. Stay Calm and Confident: On test day, stay calm and confident. Take deep breaths if you feel anxious and trust in your preparation and abilities.

13. Take Care of Yourself: Leading up to the LSAT, get enough rest, maintain a healthy diet, and engage in regular exercise. Taking care of your physical and mental well-being can positively impact your performance.

Remember that the LSAT is an essential component of your law school application, but it is not the sole factor considered by admissions committees. Combine your LSAT preparation with strong academic performance, compelling personal statements, and impactful letters of recommendation to present a well-rounded application to your desired law schools.

Financial planning and scholarships

Financial planning is a crucial aspect of preparing for law school. Law school can be expensive, and developing a solid financial plan can help you manage the costs and minimize debt. Here are some financial planning tips and strategies for law school:

1. Research Tuition and Costs: Research the tuition and other expenses associated with attending law school. Consider the cost of living in the area where the school is located.
2. Create a Budget: Develop a budget to track your income and expenses during law school. Identify areas where you can cut costs and save money.
3. Explore Scholarships and Grants: Look for scholarships and grants offered by law schools, external organizations, or private foundations. Scholarships can significantly reduce the financial burden of law school.
4. Apply for Financial Aid: Complete the Free Application for Federal Student Aid (FAFSA) to determine your eligibility for federal financial aid programs, such as loans and work-study opportunities.
5. Consider Part-Time or Online Programs: Part-time or online law school programs may offer more flexibility and can be a more cost-effective option for some students.
6. Work During Law School: Consider working part-time during law school to help cover expenses and reduce reliance on loans.
7. Limit Borrowing: Be cautious about taking on excessive student loan debt. Borrow only what is necessary to

cover tuition and living expenses.

8. Compare Loan Options: Compare loan terms, interest rates, and repayment options when considering student loans. Federal loans often offer more favorable terms than private loans.

9. Seek Out Financial Aid Advisors: Consult with financial aid advisors at your chosen law schools to explore all available financial aid options and discuss your unique financial situation.

10. Save Money Before Law School: If possible, save money before starting law school to create a financial cushion during your studies.

11. Consider Loan Forgiveness Programs: Research loan forgiveness programs for lawyers who work in public service or government positions. These programs can help manage student loan debt after graduation.

12. Negotiate Scholarships: If you receive multiple scholarship offers, consider negotiating with law schools to potentially increase scholarship amounts.

Remember that responsible financial planning can have a significant impact on your law school experience and post-graduation financial well-being. By carefully managing your finances and exploring scholarship opportunities, you can pursue your legal education with confidence and reduce financial stress during and after law school.

Surviving the First Semester

Surviving the first semester of law school can be challenging, but with the right mindset and strategies, you can navigate this critical period successfully. Here are some tips to help you thrive during your first semester of law school:

1. Stay Organized: Create a study schedule and prioritize your assignments and readings. Stay on top of deadlines and maintain a well-organized study area.

2. Attend Classes Regularly: Attend all your classes and pay attention to the professors' lectures. Taking detailed notes can help reinforce your understanding of the material.

3. Engage in Active Learning: Participate in class discussions, ask questions, and engage with the material actively. Active learning can improve comprehension and retention.

4. Prepare for Each Class: Complete all assigned readings before each class. Being prepared will enable you to follow the discussion and participate effectively.

5. Form Study Groups: Collaborate with your peers and form study groups to review class materials and discuss complex topics. Group discussions can enhance your understanding of the material.

6. Use Supplements Wisely: Utilize study aids and supplementary materials to reinforce your understanding of the subjects. However, avoid relying solely on these aids and prioritize your class notes.

7. Time Management: Manage your time efficiently to balance academic work, personal life, and self-care.

Avoid procrastination and stay disciplined in your study routine.

8. Seek Help When Needed: Don't hesitate to seek help from professors, teaching assistants, or academic advisors if you are struggling with any aspect of your studies.

9. Take Care of Yourself: Prioritize self-care and maintain a healthy lifestyle. Get enough sleep, exercise regularly, and eat nutritious meals to stay physically and mentally well.

10. Embrace the Learning Process: Law school is challenging, and it's okay to face difficulties along the way. Embrace the learning process and view challenges as opportunities for growth.

11. Focus on Understanding, Not Memorization: Instead of memorizing facts, focus on understanding the underlying concepts and legal reasoning. This approach will serve you well in exams and in practice.

12. Practice Time Management in Exams: During exams, allocate time wisely to answer each question thoroughly. Read the questions carefully and outline your answers before diving into writing.

13. Stay Positive and Persistent: Law school can be intense, but stay positive and maintain a growth mindset. Celebrate your successes and learn from any setbacks.

Remember that the first semester is an adjustment period, and it's normal to feel overwhelmed at times. Stay committed to your goals, seek support when needed, and trust in your abilities. By staying organized, engaging in active learning, and taking care of yourself, you can set the foundation for a successful law school journey. Good luck!

Embracing the Socratic method and legal reasoning

Embracing the Socratic method and legal reasoning is essential for success in law school and the legal profession. The Socratic method is a teaching technique commonly used in law schools, where professors engage students in an interactive dialogue to stimulate critical thinking and analytical skills. Here are some tips for embracing the Socratic method and developing strong legal reasoning abilities:

1. Active Engagement: Embrace the Socratic method as an opportunity to actively engage with the material and think critically about legal concepts. Listen attentively to the questions posed by professors and classmates.

2. Prepare for Class: Complete all assigned readings and prepare notes or outlines before each class. Being well-prepared will boost your confidence and ability to contribute to class discussions.

3. Think Out Loud: When called on in class, think out loud as you work through legal problems or analyze cases. Articulating your thought process allows for better understanding and fosters deeper insights.

4. Listen to Others: Pay attention to the responses and analysis offered by your classmates during Socratic exchanges. This can provide alternative perspectives and enhance your understanding of complex issues.

5. Be Open to Constructive Criticism: Embrace feedback and be open to constructive criticism from professors and peers. The Socratic method is designed to challenge

your reasoning and improve your legal analysis.

6. Analyze Legal Principles: Focus on understanding the underlying legal principles and applying them to various scenarios. Legal reasoning involves analyzing the law's application to specific facts.
7. Apply IRAC Method: Practice using the IRAC (Issue, Rule, Application, Conclusion) method to structure your legal analysis. This format helps organize your arguments in a clear and logical manner.
8. Stay Calm and Confident: Don't be afraid of making mistakes during Socratic exchanges. Stay calm and confident in your responses, even if you're unsure. Mistakes are opportunities for learning.
9. Ask Questions: Don't hesitate to ask questions when you don't fully grasp a concept. Seeking clarification shows your engagement and eagerness to learn.
10. Practice Outside of Class: Develop your legal reasoning skills outside of class through practice questions, hypotheticals, and legal writing exercises.
11. Seek Additional Resources: Consult supplementary resources, such as legal treatises, casebooks, and practice guides, to deepen your understanding of legal principles.
12. Reflect on your Progress: Regularly reflect on your progress in mastering legal reasoning and critical thinking. Identify areas for improvement and actively work on enhancing your skills.

Embracing the Socratic method and honing your legal reasoning abilities will not only benefit you in law school but also prepare you for success as a legal professional. Cultivating these skills is crucial for effective advocacy, persuasive legal writing, and sound decision-making in your future legal career.

Understanding core subjects: Contracts, Torts, and Criminal Law

Understanding core subjects such as Contracts, Torts, and Criminal Law is fundamental to the study and practice of law. These subjects form the basis of many legal principles and concepts. Here is an overview of each subject:

1. Contracts:
   - Contracts law governs the formation, interpretation, and enforcement of agreements between parties. It deals with the legal obligations and rights arising from voluntary agreements.
   - Key concepts include offer and acceptance, consideration, capacity to contract, legality, and the various types of contracts (e.g., bilateral, unilateral, implied, and express contracts).
   - Breach of contract, remedies for breach, and defenses against enforcement are also essential aspects of contracts law.

2. Torts:
   - Torts law deals with civil wrongs that cause harm or injury to individuals or their property. It provides a means for injured parties to seek compensation or damages for harm caused by others' negligence or intentional actions.
   - Common torts include negligence, intentional torts (e.g., assault, battery, defamation), strict

liability, and products liability.
- To establish a tort, one must prove the defendant's duty of care, breach of that duty, causation, and damages suffered by the plaintiff.

3. Criminal Law:
- Criminal law governs conduct that is considered harmful to society and provides for punishment and deterrence of criminal behavior.
- It includes offenses such as theft, assault, murder, fraud, and drug possession, among others.
- Criminal law operates on the principle of guilt beyond a reasonable doubt, and defendants have the right to due process and a fair trial.

In law school, these core subjects are typically covered during the first year of study and are foundational to the understanding of legal principles. Each subject involves a study of case law, statutes, and legal reasoning. Analyzing hypothetical scenarios and applying legal principles to real-world situations are essential components of learning these subjects.

For law practitioners, a solid understanding of Contracts, Torts, and Criminal Law is essential for providing legal advice, negotiating agreements, and representing clients in various legal matters. These subjects form the basis for further specialization in specific areas of law and are crucial for effective legal practice and advocacy.

Case briefing and legal analysis

Case briefing and legal analysis are essential skills in law school and the legal profession. Case briefing involves summarizing and analyzing court opinions to understand the key legal issues, holdings, and reasoning of a case. Here's a step-by-step guide on how to brief a case and conduct legal analysis:

1. Read the Case: Start by reading the case carefully and thoroughly. Identify the parties involved, the court that decided the case, and the legal issues presented.
2. Identify the Facts: Summarize the relevant facts of the case. Focus on the events and circumstances that are crucial to understanding the court's decision.
3. Determine the Issue: Identify the legal issue or question that the court had to address. The issue is the central question the court needed to resolve.
4. Review the Holding: Determine the court's decision or holding on the legal issue. This is the court's answer to the question presented.
5. Analyze the Reasoning: Examine the court's reasoning or rationale for its decision. Identify the legal principles and precedents the court relied upon to reach its conclusion.
6. Note Dissenting Opinions (If Any): Check if there are any dissenting opinions, where one or more judges disagreed with the majority. Understand the reasoning behind the dissent.
7. Create the Case Brief: Organize your findings into a case brief. A typical case brief includes the case name and citation, parties, facts, issue, holding, reasoning, and

any dissenting opinions.

Legal Analysis:

1. Apply Legal Rules: Identify and apply the relevant legal rules and principles to the facts of the case. Determine how the court's decision aligns with existing law.
2. Evaluate Policy Considerations: Consider the policy implications of the court's decision. Analyze how the ruling affects the parties involved and society as a whole.
3. Compare with Other Cases: Compare the current case with similar cases or precedents to understand how the court's decision fits within the broader legal context.
4. Consider Practical Implications: Reflect on the practical implications of the court's decision and how it may impact future cases or legal practices.
5. Formulate Legal Arguments: Use the case's legal analysis to develop legal arguments for use in legal writing, debates, or oral arguments.

Case briefing and legal analysis are crucial for law students to grasp legal principles and for practicing attorneys to provide sound legal advice, draft legal documents, and advocate effectively in court. These skills require a thorough understanding of the case law, statutory law, and legal reasoning to navigate complex legal issues and develop persuasive legal arguments.

Time management and study strategies

Time management and study strategies are vital for law students to effectively balance their academic workload and achieve success in law school. Here are some time management and study strategies that can help law students stay organized and productive:

1. Create a Study Schedule: Develop a weekly study schedule that includes dedicated time for class readings, assignments, case briefings, and review. Stick to the schedule to stay on top of your coursework.

2. Prioritize Tasks: Identify the most important tasks each day and prioritize them based on deadlines and importance. Tackle high-priority tasks first to ensure they are completed on time.

3. Use a Planner or Calendar: Utilize a planner or digital calendar to keep track of assignments, exams, and other commitments. This helps you visualize your schedule and avoid overcommitting.

4. Break Tasks into Manageable Chunks: Divide large tasks, such as reading assignments or legal research projects, into smaller, manageable parts. This approach makes the workload feel less overwhelming.

5. Set Realistic Goals: Set achievable goals for each study session or day. Celebrate your accomplishments and progress, no matter how small.

6. Avoid Procrastination: Resist the temptation to procrastinate. Start working on assignments and tasks as soon as possible to avoid last-minute stress.

7. Eliminate Distractions: Create a study environment free

from distractions. Turn off social media notifications, limit phone usage, and find a quiet space to concentrate.

8. Take Breaks: Incorporate short breaks during study sessions to recharge your mind. Taking breaks can actually enhance focus and productivity.

9. Use Active Learning Techniques: Engage actively with the material by taking notes, summarizing concepts in your own words, and discussing topics with classmates.

10. Participate in Study Groups: Join or form study groups to discuss challenging topics, exchange ideas, and reinforce your understanding of legal concepts.

11. Review and Review Again: Regularly review class notes, case briefs, and study materials to reinforce your understanding of the material and retain information effectively.

12. Practice Past Exams and Hypotheticals: Practice answering exam-style questions and hypothetical scenarios to improve your legal analysis and writing skills.

13. Seek Help When Needed: Don't hesitate to seek help from professors, teaching assistants, or academic advisors if you're struggling with any aspect of your studies.

14. Maintain a Healthy Lifestyle: Get enough sleep, eat nutritious meals, and engage in regular physical activity. A healthy lifestyle supports cognitive function and overall well-being.

By adopting effective time management and study strategies, law students can stay organized, reduce stress, and make the most of their law school experience. These skills will also be valuable throughout their legal careers for managing caseloads, meeting deadlines, and delivering high-quality work to clients.

Legal Research and Writing

Legal research and writing are critical skills for law students and legal professionals. They involve locating and analyzing legal sources and effectively communicating legal arguments in writing. Here's an overview of legal research and writing:

Legal Research:

1. Understanding Legal Research: Legal research involves finding and analyzing legal sources, such as statutes, case law, regulations, and legal commentary, to address specific legal issues.
2. Research Methods: Law students and legal professionals use various research methods, including online legal databases, law libraries, and legal research guides.
3. Identifying Relevant Sources: The key to successful legal research is identifying relevant legal sources that are applicable to the specific legal issue at hand.
4. Case Law Research: When researching case law, students examine judicial opinions to understand how courts have applied the law to specific cases.
5. Statutory Research: Statutory research involves locating and interpreting statutes and codes that govern a particular legal issue.
6. Secondary Sources: Legal research often includes consulting secondary sources, such as legal treatises, law review articles, and practice guides, to gain deeper insights into legal principles and trends.

Legal Writing:

1. Legal Writing Style: Legal writing requires a clear, concise, and formal writing style. It should be objective and free from emotional or personal opinions.
2. Writing for Different Audiences: Legal writing can vary depending on the audience, such as writing for judges, clients, or other attorneys.
3. Briefs and Memoranda: In law school, students often write legal briefs and memoranda to analyze legal issues and present legal arguments.
4. Legal Opinions: Legal professionals write legal opinions to advise clients on the application of the law to their specific situation.
5. Pleadings and Motions: Attorneys draft pleadings and motions to initiate or respond to legal actions in court.
6. Citations: Legal writing relies heavily on proper citation format, such as the Bluebook for legal citations in the United States.

Tips for Effective Legal Writing:

1. Start with an Outline: Organize your writing by creating a detailed outline to structure your arguments logically.
2. Use Clear and Precise Language: Avoid ambiguous language and use precise legal terms to convey your points accurately.
3. Support Your Arguments: Back up your legal arguments with relevant case law, statutes, and other legal authorities.
4. Edit and Revise: Carefully edit and revise your work to ensure clarity and correctness.
5. Be Objective: Legal writing should remain objective and impartial, focusing on the law and legal analysis.
6. Tailor Your Writing: Adjust your writing style and level of legal complexity to suit your audience's needs.

Legal research and writing skills are essential for law students to succeed in their coursework and for legal professionals to effectively represent clients and advocate for their positions in court. These skills are honed through practice, feedback, and a commitment to continuous improvement.

Mastering legal research techniques

Mastering legal research techniques is crucial for law students and legal professionals to effectively locate and analyze legal sources. Here are some key strategies to help you excel in legal research:

1. Understand the Legal Issue: Before starting your research, thoroughly understand the legal issue at hand. Clearly defining the research question will guide your search and prevent wasted effort on irrelevant sources.

2. Utilize Primary Sources: Primary legal sources include statutes, case law, regulations, and constitutions. Begin your research by consulting these primary sources to identify the relevant legal rules and principles.

3. Use Online Legal Databases: Online legal databases such as Westlaw, LexisNexis, and Bloomberg Law provide access to a vast collection of legal materials. Familiarize yourself with the search features and advanced search operators to refine your results.

4. Employ Boolean Search Techniques: Use Boolean operators (AND, OR, NOT) to narrow or expand your search results. Combine relevant keywords and phrases to find specific information.

5. Consult Secondary Sources: Secondary legal sources, such as legal treatises, law review articles, and practice guides, can provide valuable context, analysis, and insights on legal issues.

6. Study Legal Research Guides: Law libraries and online resources often offer legal research guides specific to certain topics or jurisdictions. These guides provide step-by-step instructions for conducting effective legal

research.

7. Check Citations and Shepardize: Verify the authority and validity of legal sources by checking the citations and Shepardizing (or KeyCiting) cases to ensure they are still good law.

8. Use Headnotes and Key Numbers: When researching case law, review headnotes and key numbers to identify relevant legal issues and related cases.

9. Explore Official Government Websites: Government websites, such as the U.S. Code and Federal Register, offer free access to primary legal sources.

10. Update Your Research: Legal materials are constantly changing, so it's essential to update your research to ensure you have the latest information and legal developments.

11. Make Use of Indexes and Table of Contents: When using legal books, start by checking the index and table of contents to locate relevant sections quickly.

12. Seek Guidance from Librarians: Librarians are valuable resources for legal research. Don't hesitate to ask for their assistance and guidance in locating relevant materials.

13. Document Your Research: Keep track of your research process and sources used. Properly cite your sources for future reference and to avoid plagiarism.

14. Practice Regularly: Legal research skills improve with practice. Make legal research an ongoing part of your study routine to enhance your proficiency.

By mastering legal research techniques, law students and legal professionals can efficiently navigate the vast body of legal information and find the authoritative sources needed to address complex legal issues. Effective legal research is a fundamental skill for success in law school and a crucial aspect of providing competent and reliable legal representation to clients.

The art of persuasive legal writing

The art of persuasive legal writing is a skill that law students and legal professionals must master to effectively advocate for their clients and present compelling legal arguments. Persuasive legal writing aims to convince the reader, whether it's a judge, opposing counsel, or client, of the strength and validity of the writer's position. Here are key strategies for achieving persuasive legal writing:

1. Know Your Audience: Understand the audience for your legal writing and tailor your arguments accordingly. Consider the judge's preferences, the opposing counsel's potential counterarguments, and the client's concerns.

2. Clear and Organized Structure: Organize your legal writing in a clear and logical manner. Use headings and subheadings to guide the reader through the argument and make it easy to follow.

3. Start with a Strong Introduction: Begin with a compelling introduction that sets the stage for your argument. Clearly state the issue and your position upfront to grab the reader's attention.

4. Present Strong Legal Analysis: Support your argument with thorough legal analysis. Cite relevant statutes, case law, and secondary sources to back up your position.

5. Address Counterarguments: Anticipate potential counterarguments and address them in your writing. Refute opposing points of view with strong reasoning and evidence.

6. Use Persuasive Language: Choose your words carefully to convey your points persuasively. Use strong and

assertive language to make your position clear.

7. Employ Rhetorical Devices: Utilize rhetorical devices such as analogies, metaphors, and rhetorical questions to make your arguments more memorable and persuasive.

8. Create Compelling Headings: Use descriptive and attention-grabbing headings to emphasize key points and draw the reader's attention.

9. Provide Practical Solutions: Offer practical and feasible solutions to the legal issues at hand. Demonstrate that your proposed course of action is the most sensible and justifiable.

10. Use Case Law Effectively: When citing case law, emphasize the most favorable cases that support your position. Distinguish unfavorable cases by explaining why they are distinguishable.

11. Write Persuasively but Ethically: Maintain ethical standards in persuasive writing. Avoid exaggeration, misrepresentation, or other unethical tactics.

12. Use Strong Conclusions: End with a strong and persuasive conclusion that summarizes your main points and reinforces your position.

13. Revise and Edit: Effective persuasive writing requires careful revision and editing. Review your work for clarity, coherence, and proper grammar.

14. Seek Feedback: Share your writing with colleagues or mentors and seek feedback. Constructive criticism can help improve your persuasive writing skills.

Persuasive legal writing is essential for legal briefs, motions, memoranda, and appellate advocacy. Mastering this skill enables legal professionals to effectively present their clients' cases, influence judicial decisions, and achieve successful outcomes in various legal contexts.

Writing case briefs and memos

Writing case briefs and memos is an integral part of legal research and analysis. Case briefs are concise summaries of court opinions, while memos are more comprehensive documents that analyze legal issues and provide recommendations. Here's how to write effective case briefs and memos:

Writing Case Briefs:

1. Case Information: Start with the case name, citation, court, and date. Include the parties involved (plaintiff and defendant).
2. Facts: Summarize the relevant facts of the case. Focus on the key events and circumstances that led to the legal dispute.
3. Issue: Identify the legal issue or question that the court had to address. The issue is the central question the court needed to resolve.
4. Holding: State the court's decision or holding on the legal issue. This is the court's answer to the question presented.
5. Reasoning: Analyze the court's reasoning or rationale for its decision. Identify the legal principles and precedents the court relied upon to reach its conclusion.
6. Rule of Law: Extract the legal rule or principle established by the court's decision. This is the legal principle that governs similar cases in the future.
7. Concise Format: Keep your case briefs concise, focusing on the essential information and omitting unnecessary details.

Writing Memos:

1. Heading: Include a heading with the names of the sender and recipient, date, and a concise subject line.
2. Issue Statement: Clearly state the legal issue or question that the memo aims to address.
3. Facts: Provide a brief summary of the relevant facts of the case or legal matter. Only include essential details necessary for the analysis.
4. Legal Analysis: Conduct a comprehensive legal analysis of the issue at hand. Use relevant statutes, case law, and secondary sources to support your analysis.
5. Application: Apply the legal principles to the facts of the case or legal scenario. Explain how the law should be applied to the specific situation.
6. Discussion: Present a detailed discussion of the arguments and counterarguments related to the legal issue. Address potential weaknesses and strengths of each argument.
7. Conclusion and Recommendation: Summarize the main points of the memo and provide a clear recommendation or course of action based on your legal analysis.
8. Citations: Properly cite all legal authorities and sources used in the memo using the appropriate citation style (e.g., Bluebook).
9. Proofread and Edit: Review the memo for clarity, coherence, and accuracy. Edit for grammar, spelling, and formatting errors.
10. Reader-Friendly Format: Use headings, bullet points, and numbered lists to organize the memo and make it easy to read.

Writing case briefs and memos effectively requires attention to detail, legal analysis, and concise writing. These skills are valuable for law students to excel in their coursework and for legal professionals to communicate legal analysis and recommendations to clients and colleagues.

Effective use of legal citations

Effective use of legal citations is crucial in legal writing to provide a clear and authoritative reference to legal sources. Proper citations lend credibility to your arguments, allow readers to verify your research, and demonstrate your understanding of the relevant legal authorities. Here are some tips for using legal citations effectively:

1. Use the Correct Citation Format: Follow the required citation format for your jurisdiction or court, such as the Bluebook for legal citations in the United States. Consistency and accuracy in citation style are essential.

2. Cite Primary and Secondary Sources: Include citations to primary legal sources (e.g., cases, statutes, regulations) and secondary sources (e.g., law review articles, legal treatises) to support your legal analysis.

3. Pinpoint Citations: Use pinpoint citations to refer to specific pages, paragraphs, or sections of a legal source where the relevant information can be found. This helps readers locate the exact passage you are referencing.

4. Short Form Citations: After providing a full citation in the first instance, use short form citations for subsequent references to the same source. Short form citations typically include the author's name, short title, and page number.

5. Parallel Citations: Provide parallel citations when referencing multiple sources that cite the same case or statute. Include the most authoritative citation first, followed by other parallel citations.

6. Signal Phrases: Integrate citations smoothly into your

sentences using signal phrases, such as "according to," "as stated in," or "see also." This connects the citation to your analysis seamlessly.

7. Quotations and Block Quotes: When using direct quotes, include the page number in the citation. For block quotes, use ellipses (...) to indicate omitted text within the quotation.

8. Parenthetical Explanations: Use parenthetical explanations to provide additional context or information about the cited source, especially when the citation is not self-explanatory.

9. Update Citations: Ensure that all citations are up-to-date and still good law. Shepardize or KeyCite your sources to verify their current validity.

10. Check Cross-References: When referencing multiple authorities, verify that cross-references are accurate and lead to the correct sources.

11. Avoid Over-Citation: Use citations judiciously. Over-citation can clutter your writing and distract from your arguments.

12. Verify Citations in the Final Draft: During the editing process, double-check all citations to ensure they are correct and properly formatted.

Effective legal citations add credibility and authority to your legal writing. Following these guidelines will help you use legal citations effectively, making your legal arguments more persuasive and reliable.

Balancing Academic and Personal Life

Balancing academic and personal life is a challenge faced by many students, including those pursuing legal education. Achieving this balance is essential for maintaining overall well-being and academic success. Here are some tips for finding a balance between academic commitments and personal life:

1. Time Management: Develop a schedule or to-do list to allocate time for both academic tasks and personal activities. Prioritize important tasks and set realistic deadlines.

2. Create a Study Routine: Establish a consistent study routine that includes dedicated study hours and breaks. This will help you stay focused and avoid procrastination.

3. Set Boundaries: Learn to say no to unnecessary commitments that can interfere with your study and personal time. Setting boundaries will allow you to manage your time more effectively.

4. Utilize Breaks Wisely: Use breaks between classes or study sessions for relaxation and personal activities. Taking short breaks can boost productivity and prevent burnout.

5. Plan Leisure Activities: Schedule leisure activities, hobbies, and social events in advance. Having planned time for relaxation will help you unwind and maintain a healthy balance.

6. Stay Organized: Keep your study materials and personal belongings organized to save time and reduce stress.

7. Seek Support: Reach out to friends, family, or academic

advisors for support and guidance. They can provide valuable insights and help you stay on track.

8. Practice Self-Care: Take care of your physical and mental health by getting enough sleep, eating well, and engaging in activities that help you relax and de-stress.

9. Join Study Groups: Consider forming study groups with classmates. Working together can make studying more enjoyable and efficient.

10. Be Realistic: Set realistic expectations for yourself. It's okay to seek help if you're struggling with academic or personal challenges.

11. Stay Active: Engage in physical activities, such as exercise or sports, to maintain energy levels and reduce stress.

12. Find Flexibility: Be open to adjusting your schedule when unexpected events arise. Flexibility is essential for maintaining balance in a dynamic environment.

13. Celebrate Achievements: Acknowledge and celebrate your academic achievements and personal milestones to stay motivated.

14. Reflect and Reassess: Regularly assess how you're managing your time and make adjustments as needed. Reflecting on your progress will help you improve your balance over time.

Balancing academic and personal life requires intentional effort and adaptability. By implementing these strategies, you can achieve a healthier balance and excel both academically and personally. Remember that finding the right balance is an ongoing process, and it's essential to be kind to yourself throughout the journey.

Managing stress and avoiding burnout

Managing stress and avoiding burnout is crucial for law students and legal professionals, as the legal profession can be demanding and stressful. Here are some strategies to effectively manage stress and prevent burnout:

1. Identify Stress Triggers: Recognize the factors that cause stress and anxiety in your life. Understanding your stress triggers can help you develop coping strategies.
2. Practice Mindfulness and Meditation: Engage in mindfulness techniques and meditation to promote relaxation and reduce stress levels.
3. Exercise Regularly: Incorporate regular physical activity into your routine. Exercise has numerous benefits for both physical and mental well-being.
4. Take Breaks: Schedule regular breaks during study or work sessions. Short breaks can help you recharge and maintain focus.
5. Seek Social Support: Share your feelings and experiences with friends, family, or colleagues. Social support can provide emotional relief and a sense of connection.
6. Set Realistic Goals: Set achievable and manageable goals for yourself. Avoid overwhelming yourself with unrealistic expectations.
7. Time Management: Use effective time management techniques to prioritize tasks and avoid last-minute rushes.
8. Delegate Tasks: Learn to delegate tasks when possible, whether it's academic work or professional responsibilities.

9. Limit Caffeine and Sugar Intake: Reduce the consumption of caffeine and sugary foods, as they can contribute to stress and anxiety.
10. Sleep Well: Prioritize getting enough sleep each night to improve focus, concentration, and overall well-being.
11. Practice Breathing Exercises: Deep breathing exercises can help calm the nervous system and reduce stress.
12. Engage in Relaxing Activities: Participate in activities that you enjoy and find relaxing, such as reading, listening to music, or spending time in nature.
13. Seek Professional Help: If stress becomes overwhelming or affects your well-being, consider seeking support from a counselor or therapist.
14. Create Boundaries: Set clear boundaries between work or study time and personal time. Avoid bringing work-related stress into your personal life.
15. Celebrate Achievements: Acknowledge and celebrate your accomplishments, no matter how small. Positive reinforcement can boost motivation.
16. Maintain a Healthy Work-Life Balance: Strive for a healthy balance between academic or professional commitments and personal life.
17. Engage in Hobbies: Pursue hobbies or activities outside of work or study to foster a sense of fulfillment and relaxation.
18. Practice Self-Compassion: Be kind to yourself and avoid self-criticism. Recognize that everyone experiences stress, and it's okay to take breaks and seek support.

Remember that stress management is a personal journey, and different strategies work for different individuals. It's essential to find what works best for you and to prioritize self-care to maintain overall well-being and prevent burnout.

Time management and organization skills

Time management and organization skills are critical for law students and legal professionals to handle their academic and professional responsibilities efficiently. Here are some effective time management and organization strategies:

1. Prioritize Tasks: Identify the most important and time-sensitive tasks and prioritize them on your to-do list.
2. Create a Schedule: Develop a daily or weekly schedule that includes study or work hours, breaks, and personal time.
3. Use a Planner or Calendar: Utilize a physical planner, digital calendar, or time management app to track deadlines, appointments, and commitments.
4. Set Realistic Goals: Set achievable and realistic goals for each day or week. Breaking tasks into smaller, manageable parts can help you stay focused and motivated.
5. Avoid Procrastination: Take action promptly and avoid delaying tasks. Procrastination can lead to unnecessary stress and overwhelm.
6. Manage Distractions: Minimize distractions during study or work time. Turn off notifications and find a quiet place to concentrate.
7. Batch Similar Tasks: Group similar tasks together and complete them in batches. This can improve efficiency and save time.
8. Use Time Blocking: Allocate specific time blocks for different activities, such as studying, research, and personal time.

9. Take Regular Breaks: Schedule short breaks during study or work sessions to recharge and maintain productivity.
10. Delegate When Possible: Delegate tasks to others if it's appropriate and possible. This can free up time for more critical responsibilities.
11. Review Progress: Regularly review your progress and assess whether you're on track with your goals and schedule.
12. Organize Study Materials: Keep study materials and legal research well-organized, whether in physical files or digital folders.
13. Use Checklists: Create checklists for tasks and assignments to ensure nothing is overlooked.
14. Be Flexible: Be open to adjusting your schedule and plans when unexpected events arise.
15. Eliminate Time-Wasting Activities: Identify and minimize activities that consume excessive time without contributing to your goals.
16. Learn to Say No: Avoid overcommitting yourself and be selective about taking on additional responsibilities.
17. Set Deadlines: Set personal deadlines for tasks to stay accountable and avoid last-minute rushes.
18. Avoid Multitasking: Focus on one task at a time to enhance productivity and the quality of your work.
19. Review and Reflect: At the end of the day or week, review your accomplishments and evaluate areas for improvement.
20. Practice Self-Care: Ensure you get enough rest, exercise, and relaxation to maintain a clear mind and sustained energy.

Developing strong time management and organization skills takes practice and self-discipline. By implementing these strategies consistently, law students and legal professionals can better manage their time, reduce stress, and enhance their overall productivity and success.

Finding a support network and seeking help when needed

Finding a support network and seeking help when needed is essential for law students and legal professionals to navigate the challenges of their academic and professional journey. Here are some ways to build a support network and seek help effectively:

1. Connect with Classmates: Form study groups or join student organizations to connect with classmates who can provide academic and emotional support.
2. Reach Out to Professors: Develop a professional relationship with your professors. They can offer guidance, mentorship, and clarification on course material.
3. Utilize Academic Advisors: Consult with academic advisors to discuss academic goals, course selections, and any challenges you may be facing.
4. Seek Peer Mentoring: Engage in peer mentoring programs to connect with experienced students who can offer insights and advice.
5. Attend Workshops and Seminars: Participate in workshops and seminars on time management, stress reduction, and other relevant topics to gain valuable skills and knowledge.
6. Join Professional Associations: Become a member of legal or professional associations to expand your network and access resources and career opportunities.
7. Reach Out to Career Services: Use your law school's career services office for guidance on internships, job

searches, and career development.

8. Connect with Alumni: Network with alumni to gain insights into the legal profession, job prospects, and career paths.
9. Join Online Forums: Participate in online forums or social media groups for law students and legal professionals to seek advice and support.
10. Attend Networking Events: Attend networking events and conferences to build connections with professionals in the legal field.
11. Family and Friends: Lean on your family and friends for emotional support and encouragement during challenging times.
12. Seek Mental Health Support: If you're experiencing significant stress or mental health concerns, don't hesitate to seek help from counselors or therapists.
13. Utilize Professional Resources: Access resources such as legal research databases, library services, and writing centers to enhance your academic performance.
14. Discuss Concerns Early: If you encounter academic difficulties or other challenges, discuss them with professors or advisors early on to explore possible solutions.
15. Collaborate with Colleagues: In a legal practice setting, collaborate with colleagues and senior attorneys to learn and grow professionally.
16. Attend Continuing Education Programs: Engage in continuing legal education programs to expand your knowledge and stay updated on legal developments.
17. Volunteer or Pro Bono Work: Participate in pro bono work or volunteering to make a positive impact and connect with like-minded individuals.

Remember that seeking help is a sign of strength, not weakness. Building a support network and seeking assistance when needed will not only enhance your academic and professional success but also contribute to your overall well-being and personal growth as a law student or legal professional.

Prioritizing self-care and well-being

Prioritizing self-care and well-being is crucial for law students and legal professionals to maintain their physical and mental health while navigating the demands of their academic and professional responsibilities. Here are some strategies to prioritize self-care:

1. Establish a Balanced Routine: Create a daily or weekly routine that includes time for studying, work, relaxation, exercise, and personal activities.
2. Get Adequate Sleep: Aim for 7-9 hours of quality sleep each night to support cognitive function and overall well-being.
3. Eat Nutritious Foods: Maintain a balanced diet with plenty of fruits, vegetables, whole grains, and protein to fuel your body and mind.
4. Engage in Regular Exercise: Incorporate physical activity into your routine to reduce stress and improve mood.
5. Take Breaks: Allow yourself regular breaks during study or work sessions to rest and recharge.
6. Practice Mindfulness and Meditation: Engage in mindfulness techniques and meditation to reduce stress and increase self-awareness.
7. Limit Screen Time: Reduce excessive screen time, especially before bedtime, to improve sleep quality.
8. Engage in Hobbies and Relaxation Activities: Set aside time for hobbies and activities that bring you joy and relaxation.
9. Seek Emotional Support: Share your feelings and

experiences with friends, family, or a counselor to process emotions and reduce stress.

10. Set Boundaries: Establish clear boundaries between work or study time and personal time to prevent burnout.
11. Learn to Say No: Avoid overcommitting yourself and prioritize activities that align with your values and well-being.
12. Practice Gratitude: Take time to reflect on the positive aspects of your life and express gratitude regularly.
13. Spend Time Outdoors: Spend time in nature to recharge and improve mental well-being.
14. Disconnect from Technology: Unplug from digital devices periodically to reduce distractions and promote mindfulness.
15. Seek Help When Needed: If you're experiencing significant stress or mental health concerns, don't hesitate to seek professional support.
16. Engage in Acts of Kindness: Doing something kind for others can improve your mood and overall well-being.
17. Practice Self-Compassion: Be kind to yourself and avoid self-criticism during challenging times.
18. Schedule Personal Time: Prioritize personal time for self-care activities, hobbies, and relaxation.
19. Reflect and Assess: Regularly assess your well-being and self-care practices, and make adjustments as needed.
20. Make Self-Care a Habit: Incorporate self-care activities into your routine consistently to make them a habit.

Prioritizing self-care is not a luxury but a necessity for maintaining physical and mental health. By incorporating these strategies into your daily life, you can enhance your overall well-being and better manage the challenges of law school and legal practice. Remember that taking care of yourself is essential for being the best version of yourself both academically and professionally.

Building Professional Connections

Building professional connections is essential for law students and legal professionals to expand their network, explore career opportunities, and enhance their professional growth. Here are some strategies for building and nurturing professional connections:

1. Attend Networking Events: Participate in legal conferences, seminars, and networking events to meet fellow law students and professionals in the legal field.
2. Join Professional Associations: Become a member of legal or professional associations relevant to your interests and practice areas.
3. Utilize Social Media: Connect with legal professionals on platforms like LinkedIn and Twitter to stay updated on industry news and trends.
4. Alumni Network: Engage with your law school's alumni network to access mentorship and job opportunities.
5. Informational Interviews: Request informational interviews with experienced attorneys or legal professionals to gain insights into their career paths.
6. Volunteer or Pro Bono Work: Participate in pro bono work or volunteer opportunities to meet like-minded professionals and make a positive impact.
7. Engage with Faculty: Establish relationships with professors and legal faculty who can offer guidance and recommendations.
8. Internships and Clerkships: Seek internships or clerkships to gain practical experience and build connections within legal organizations.

9. Be Genuine and Respectful: Approach networking with sincerity and respect, showing genuine interest in others' experiences and perspectives.

10. Follow Up: After networking events or meetings, follow up with a brief thank-you email to express appreciation and reinforce the connection.

11. Offer Assistance: Be willing to help others with their professional needs or projects, as reciprocity is an essential aspect of networking.

12. Attend CLE Programs: Participate in continuing legal education programs to network with experienced attorneys and industry experts.

13. Online Communities: Join online forums and legal communities to engage in discussions and connect with professionals worldwide.

14. Collaborate on Projects: Seek opportunities to collaborate on legal projects or research papers with peers or professionals.

15. Build Your Personal Brand: Establish a professional online presence and showcase your expertise through blog posts, articles, or thought leadership.

16. Be Active in Bar Associations: Participate in local or state bar association events and committees to connect with legal professionals in your region.

17. Offer to Speak or Present: Volunteer to speak at conferences or events to demonstrate your expertise and broaden your network.

18. Attend Law Firm Receptions: If possible, attend law firm receptions or open houses to interact with attorneys from different practice areas.

19. Join Mentorship Programs: Seek out formal or informal mentorship programs to gain guidance from experienced professionals.

20. Follow Up Regularly: Stay in touch with your connections regularly, whether through occasional emails or meetings, to maintain relationships.

Building professional connections is an ongoing process, and the more effort and authenticity you put into it, the more meaningful and beneficial your network will become. Remember that networking is about building relationships, and approaching it with a positive and open mindset will lead to fruitful connections and opportunities in the legal field.

The importance of networking in the legal profession

Networking plays a crucial role in the legal profession and offers numerous benefits for law students and legal professionals alike. Here are some reasons why networking is essential in the legal profession:

1. Career Opportunities: Networking provides access to job openings, internships, clerkships, and other career opportunities that may not be publicly advertised.
2. Building a Professional Reputation: By networking, you can showcase your skills, expertise, and knowledge, leading to a positive professional reputation among peers and potential employers.
3. Referrals and Recommendations: Building strong professional connections increases the likelihood of receiving referrals and recommendations from trusted colleagues, mentors, or supervisors.
4. Mentorship and Guidance: Networking allows you to connect with experienced attorneys who can offer valuable mentorship and guidance throughout your legal career.
5. Industry Insights: Through networking events and discussions, you can gain insights into current legal trends, changes in the legal landscape, and emerging practice areas.
6. Access to Knowledge and Resources: Networking provides access to legal research, resources, and best practices shared by seasoned professionals.

7. Professional Development: Interacting with other legal professionals helps to develop critical skills, such as communication, negotiation, and teamwork.

8. Business Development: For legal practitioners in private practice, networking is essential for business development and gaining new clients.

9. Support System: Networking can create a supportive community of like-minded professionals who understand the challenges and demands of the legal profession.

10. Enhancing Communication Skills: Regular networking opportunities allow for honing communication and interpersonal skills necessary for effective legal practice.

11. Collaboration Opportunities: Networking opens doors for potential collaboration on legal projects, research papers, or joint ventures with peers and colleagues.

12. Staying Updated: Engaging with other legal professionals helps you stay updated on changes in laws, regulations, and case law.

13. Professional Confidence: Developing a strong network can boost your professional confidence, making it easier to navigate legal challenges and opportunities.

14. Access to Continuing Education: Networking events often feature continuing legal education programs, allowing you to enhance your legal knowledge and expertise.

15. Personal Growth: Networking exposes you to diverse perspectives and experiences, fostering personal growth and development.

16. Recognition and Visibility: Active networking can increase your visibility in the legal community, leading to recognition for your achievements and contributions.

17. Long-Term Relationships: Building long-term relationships through networking can lead to collaborative projects and career advancements over time.

18. Emotional Support: Networking provides an avenue to discuss challenges and seek emotional support from individuals who understand the legal profession's demands.

In the competitive legal landscape, networking is not just about meeting people but about cultivating meaningful connections. A strong network can serve as a valuable resource throughout your legal career, facilitating professional growth, personal development, and success in the legal profession.

Building relationships with professors and peers

Building relationships with professors and peers is essential for law students to create a supportive and enriching learning environment. These relationships can also lead to valuable mentorship, networking opportunities, and academic and career guidance. Here are some tips for building strong relationships with professors and peers:

With Professors:

1. Attend Office Hours: Regularly attend professors' office hours to discuss course material, seek clarification, and show your interest in the subject matter.
2. Participate in Class: Engage actively in class discussions, answer questions, and ask thoughtful questions to demonstrate your commitment to learning.
3. Be Respectful and Professional: Treat professors with respect and professionalism, both inside and outside the classroom.
4. Seek Feedback: Request feedback on assignments and exams to understand your strengths and areas for improvement.
5. Show Interest in Their Work: Familiarize yourself with professors' research or publications and ask them about their academic interests.
6. Follow Up on Discussions: If a professor mentions a topic of interest during class, follow up with them later to continue the discussion.

7. Offer Assistance: If appropriate, offer your assistance in research projects or other academic endeavors.

With Peers:

1. Join Study Groups: Form or join study groups with classmates to collaborate on course material and share study strategies.
2. Attend Social Events: Participate in social events or gatherings organized by your law school or student organizations to get to know your peers in a more relaxed setting.
3. Be Approachable and Friendly: Be open to making new friends and approachable to others who may want to connect with you.
4. Collaborate on Projects: Work together on group assignments and projects to foster teamwork and camaraderie.
5. Share Resources: Share class notes, study guides, or helpful resources with your peers.
6. Respect Differences: Law school brings together individuals with diverse backgrounds and perspectives. Respect and appreciate these differences.
7. Offer Support: Be supportive and empathetic towards your peers during challenging times or stressful periods.

General Tips:

1. Be Genuine: Be authentic and true to yourself in your interactions with professors and peers.
2. Listen Actively: Practice active listening during conversations to show genuine interest in what others have to say.
3. Be Reliable: Be dependable and follow through on any commitments you make.
4. Follow Professional Etiquette: Observe professional

etiquette in all interactions, whether in person, email, or virtual meetings.

5. Maintain Balance: While building relationships is important, balance your social interactions with your academic responsibilities.

6. Show Appreciation: Express gratitude to professors and peers who offer guidance or support.

7. Stay Positive: Approach interactions with a positive attitude and a willingness to learn and grow.

Building meaningful relationships with professors and peers is a gradual process that requires consistent effort and genuine interest in others. These connections can enrich your law school experience and lay the foundation for a strong professional network in the legal field.

Engaging with legal professionals and alumni

Engaging with legal professionals and alumni is a valuable aspect of a law student's journey and can provide numerous benefits for career development and networking. Here are some strategies to effectively engage with legal professionals and alumni:

1. Attend Networking Events: Participate in legal conferences, seminars, workshops, and alumni gatherings to meet legal professionals and alumni from different practice areas.
2. Join Professional Associations: Become a member of legal or alumni associations relevant to your interests and practice areas.
3. Alumni Network: Connect with your law school's alumni network through online platforms or alumni events to access mentorship and job opportunities.
4. Informational Interviews: Request informational interviews with experienced attorneys or alumni to gain insights into their career paths and experiences.
5. Internships and Clerkships: Seek internships or clerkships to gain practical experience and build connections within legal organizations.
6. Utilize Social Media: Connect with legal professionals and alumni on platforms like LinkedIn to stay updated on industry news and trends.
7. Attend Law Firm Receptions: If possible, attend law firm receptions or open houses to interact with attorneys from different practice areas.
8. Engage with Law School Events: Participate in law school events that involve alumni, such as panel

discussions, career fairs, and networking receptions.

9. Follow Legal Blogs and Publications: Read legal blogs and publications to stay informed about legal developments and potential conversation starters with legal professionals.

10. Offer Assistance: If you have skills or expertise that can be helpful to legal professionals or alumni, offer your assistance or support.

11. Collaborate on Projects: Seek opportunities to collaborate on legal projects, research papers, or volunteer activities with legal professionals and alumni.

12. Follow Up and Stay Connected: After networking events or meetings, follow up with a thank-you email and stay connected with legal professionals and alumni through occasional updates.

13. Volunteer and Pro Bono Work: Engage in pro bono work or volunteer opportunities to connect with legal professionals who are passionate about giving back to the community.

14. Seek Mentorship: If possible, seek out formal or informal mentorship from legal professionals or alumni who can provide guidance and support.

15. Attend Continuing Legal Education (CLE) Programs: Participate in CLE programs to expand your legal knowledge and network with experienced attorneys.

16. Ask for Recommendations: If you have worked closely with legal professionals or alumni, consider asking for recommendations or testimonials for your professional profile.

17. Show Interest in Their Work: Show genuine interest in the work and accomplishments of legal professionals and alumni during conversations.

18. Be Respectful and Professional: Treat legal professionals and alumni with respect and professionalism, as you would with professors and peers.

19. Express Gratitude: Express appreciation to legal

professionals and alumni who offer guidance, support, or opportunities.

20. Be Proactive: Take the initiative to reach out to legal professionals and alumni, and be proactive in building and maintaining these relationships.

Engaging with legal professionals and alumni is an ongoing process that requires active involvement and a genuine interest in others' experiences and careers. These connections can provide valuable insights, mentorship, and potential career opportunities as you progress in your legal journey.

Leveraging social media for professional development

Social media platforms offer numerous opportunities for law students and legal professionals to enhance their professional development and networking. Here are some ways to leverage social media for professional growth:

1. LinkedIn: Create a professional LinkedIn profile showcasing your legal skills, experience, and accomplishments. Connect with legal professionals, alumni, and potential employers. Join legal groups and participate in discussions to stay updated on industry trends and network with like-minded individuals.
2. Twitter: Follow legal experts, law firms, and legal publications on Twitter to receive real-time updates on legal news and developments. Engage in legal conversations using relevant hashtags to contribute to discussions and build your online presence.
3. Legal Blogs and Publications: Follow reputable legal blogs and publications on platforms like Medium, WordPress, or Bloglovin to access insightful articles, comment on posts, and engage with authors and contributors.
4. YouTube: Subscribe to legal channels or channels of prominent legal professionals to watch educational videos, webinars, and interviews related to law practice and legal developments.
5. Instagram: Follow legal organizations and professionals on Instagram to get a behind-the-scenes look at legal

events, workshops, and conferences. Use Instagram Stories and posts to share your legal experiences and interests.

6. Facebook Groups: Join law-related Facebook groups to connect with fellow law students and legal professionals, ask questions, and share insights.

7. Legal Podcasts: Listen to legal podcasts to expand your knowledge, hear from legal experts, and gain insights into various legal topics and practice areas.

8. Professional Networking Events: Stay updated on upcoming legal networking events, webinars, and virtual conferences through social media announcements and event pages.

9. Social Media Discussions: Engage in respectful and constructive discussions on legal topics, news, and court decisions to showcase your legal knowledge and critical thinking skills.

10. Online Courses and Webinars: Look out for online courses and webinars shared on social media platforms, which can help you develop new legal skills and expertise.

11. Personal Branding: Use social media platforms to build a positive personal brand by sharing content related to your legal interests, achievements, and career goals.

12. Follow Legal Influencers: Identify and follow legal influencers or thought leaders on social media who share valuable insights and perspectives on the legal profession.

13. Virtual Internships: Use social media to explore virtual internship opportunities and connect with legal organizations offering remote internships.

14. Online Workshops and Seminars: Keep an eye out for online workshops and seminars on social media platforms that can help you improve your legal skills and knowledge.

15. Share Legal Resources: Share relevant legal articles, blog

posts, and webinars with your network to establish yourself as a valuable source of legal information.

Remember to maintain a professional and respectful online presence, as social media can impact your professional reputation. Balance your use of social media for professional development with privacy settings and be mindful of what you share publicly. By leveraging social media effectively, law students and legal professionals can build a strong online presence, expand their networks, and stay informed about the latest legal developments and opportunities.

Preparing for Exams

Preparing for exams is an essential part of a law student's journey. Effective exam preparation involves a combination of organization, time management, and study strategies. Here are some tips to help you prepare for law school exams:

1. Understand the Exam Format: Familiarize yourself with the format of the exams, including the types of questions, time limits, and weighting of different sections.
2. Create a Study Schedule: Develop a study schedule that allocates sufficient time for each subject or topic. Break down the material into manageable study sessions.
3. Review Class Notes: Regularly review your class notes and readings to reinforce your understanding of the material covered in lectures and readings.
4. Outline and Summarize: Create outlines or summaries of key concepts, cases, and principles for each subject. This will help you organize your thoughts and condense complex information.
5. Practice with Sample Questions: Use past exams or sample questions provided by professors to practice answering different types of exam questions.
6. Work in Study Groups: Collaborate with study groups to discuss concepts, quiz each other, and gain different perspectives on legal issues.
7. Use Flashcards: Create flashcards with legal terms, case names, and key principles to aid in memory retention and quick review.
8. Seek Clarification: If you have questions or uncertainties

about any material, seek clarification from professors or teaching assistants.

9. Take Breaks: Schedule regular breaks during study sessions to avoid burnout and maintain focus.

10. Simulate Exam Conditions: Practice answering exam questions under timed conditions to simulate the pressure of the actual exam.

11. Identify Weak Areas: Assess your strengths and weaknesses in each subject and focus additional time on areas that need improvement.

12. Review Sample Answers: After completing practice exams, review sample answers or model answers provided by professors to understand the expected level of analysis and depth.

13. Practice Issue Spotting: Develop the skill of issue spotting, which is crucial for answering legal questions accurately.

14. Stay Organized: Keep your study materials, notes, and outlines organized to facilitate efficient study sessions.

15. Seek Feedback: If your law school offers exam review sessions or opportunities to discuss exam performance with professors, take advantage of them to gain insights into your exam strategies.

16. Manage Stress: Adopt stress-reduction techniques such as exercise, meditation, or hobbies to maintain a balanced approach to exam preparation.

17. Focus on Understanding: Instead of memorizing information, focus on understanding the underlying principles and reasoning behind legal concepts.

18. Practice Active Learning: Engage actively with the material by asking questions, making connections, and applying legal concepts to real-world scenarios.

Remember that exam preparation is a gradual process, and consistency is key. Start early, stay organized, and be disciplined in your study habits. With effective preparation, you can approach law school exams with confidence and maximize your chances of success.

Strategies for effective exam preparation

Effective exam preparation requires a well-organized and disciplined approach. Here are some strategies to help you prepare for exams successfully:

1. Start Early: Begin your exam preparation well in advance to allow sufficient time to cover all the material thoroughly.
2. Create a Study Plan: Develop a study schedule that outlines what subjects or topics you will study each day and the time allotted for each.
3. Prioritize: Identify the most important or challenging subjects and prioritize them in your study plan.
4. Break Down the Material: Divide the material into smaller, manageable chunks and study one topic at a time.
5. Use Active Learning Techniques: Engage with the material actively by summarizing, asking questions, and teaching concepts to others.
6. Develop Study Guides: Create study guides, outlines, or flashcards to review and consolidate key information.
7. Review Class Notes Regularly: Consistently review your class notes and readings to reinforce your understanding of the material.
8. Practice with Sample Questions: Use past exams, sample questions, or practice quizzes to test your knowledge and improve your exam-taking skills.
9. Join Study Groups: Collaborate with study groups to discuss concepts, quiz each other, and gain different perspectives on legal issues.

10. Simulate Exam Conditions: Practice answering exam questions under timed conditions to get accustomed to the time constraints.
11. Use Memory Techniques: Employ mnemonic devices or memory techniques to remember complex legal principles and case names.
12. Take Short Breaks: Schedule short breaks during study sessions to rest and recharge your mind.
13. Get Enough Sleep: Prioritize restful sleep to enhance memory retention and cognitive function.
14. Seek Clarification: If you have questions or uncertainties about any material, seek clarification from professors or teaching assistants.
15. Review Model Answers: After completing practice exams, review model answers or sample answers provided by professors to understand the expected level of analysis and depth.
16. Test Yourself: Quiz yourself on key concepts to identify areas that need further review.
17. Stay Focused and Avoid Procrastination: Minimize distractions and stay focused during study sessions. Avoid procrastination by sticking to your study plan.
18. Stay Healthy: Maintain a balanced diet, exercise regularly, and practice stress-reduction techniques to support your overall well-being during exam preparation.
19. Revise Weak Areas: Assess your strengths and weaknesses in each subject and dedicate additional time to areas that need improvement.
20. Reward Yourself: Set small, achievable goals and reward yourself when you accomplish them to stay motivated.

Remember that effective exam preparation involves consistent effort and a positive mindset. Be patient with yourself and trust in your abilities. By following these strategies, you can approach exams with confidence and perform at your best.

Outlining and review techniques

Outlining and review are essential study techniques that help law students organize and consolidate the material they have learned. Here are some strategies for effective outlining and review:

1. Creating Outlines: a. Use a Hierarchical Structure: Organize your outline in a hierarchical manner, with main topics and subtopics clearly defined. b. Include Key Concepts: Include key legal concepts, principles, rules, and case names in your outline. c. Condense Information: Summarize lengthy cases and readings into concise points in your outline. d. Use Headings and Formatting: Use headings, bullet points, and formatting to make your outline visually clear and easy to navigate. e. Use Abbreviations: Develop a system of abbreviations and shorthand to save time and space in your outline.

2. Reviewing Outlines: a. Regular Review: Review your outlines regularly to reinforce your understanding of the material. b. Active Review: Engage with the material actively during review by asking questions and quizzing yourself on key concepts. c. Use Flashcards: Create flashcards based on your outline to test your memory and recall important legal principles. d. Teach the Material: Teach the material to a study partner or yourself to solidify your understanding and improve retention. e. Compare with Class Notes: Cross-reference your outline with your class notes to ensure you haven't missed any important information.

3. Flow Charts and Diagrams: a. Use Flow Charts: Create flow charts or diagrams to visually represent complex

legal processes or analysis. b. Visual Learning: Visual aids can help you understand how legal concepts connect and flow together.

4. Cornell Method: a. Use the Cornell Method during class lectures and while reviewing your outlines. b. Summarize: Summarize key points, legal principles, and case names in the main column of your notes. c. Keywords and Questions: Use the left column to write down keywords and questions that prompt your understanding of the material. d. Summary Section: Write a summary of the main points at the bottom of the page after the lecture or review session.

5. Mind Mapping: a. Use mind maps to visually organize legal concepts and relationships. b. Central Topic: Start with a central topic and branch out with subtopics and supporting details.

6. Practice with Sample Questions: a. Use practice exams or sample questions to test your understanding of the material and apply your knowledge. b. Analyze Model Answers: Review model answers to understand how to structure your responses effectively.

7. Group Study: a. Organize study groups where you can share and compare outlines and quiz each other on legal concepts.

Remember that outlining and review techniques are not one-size-fits-all, so experiment with different methods to find what works best for you. Consistency in outlining and regular review will help reinforce your knowledge, improve retention, and prepare you for law school exams successfully.

Practice exams and mock sessions

Practice exams and mock sessions are valuable tools for law students to enhance their exam preparation and improve their performance. Here's how you can make the most of practice exams and mock sessions:

1. Obtain Past Exams: Obtain past exams from professors or law school resources to simulate the actual exam experience.
2. Set Timed Conditions: Take practice exams under timed conditions to replicate the pressure and time constraints of the real exam.
3. Use Exam Techniques: Apply the exam techniques you have learned, such as issue spotting, rule synthesis, and effective writing.
4. Review Model Answers: After completing practice exams, review model answers or sample answers provided by professors to understand the expected level of analysis and writing style.
5. Seek Feedback: If your law school offers exam review sessions, attend them to get feedback on your exam responses and identify areas for improvement.
6. Engage in Mock Sessions: Organize mock sessions with study partners or classmates to practice answering exam questions and receive constructive feedback.
7. Analyze Weak Areas: Identify weak areas in your exam responses and focus additional study time on improving those areas.
8. Simulate Exam Environment: Try to simulate the exam environment as closely as possible during practice

exams and mock sessions. Sit at a desk, turn off distractions, and adhere to the time limit.

9. Vary Practice Questions: Use a variety of practice questions, including multiple-choice, essay, and problem-solving questions, to enhance your exam skills.

10. Focus on Exam Structure: Pay attention to the structure of your exam responses, including clear introductions, well-organized body paragraphs, and concise conclusions.

11. Emphasize Issue Spotting: Practice issue spotting to quickly identify the legal issues presented in exam questions.

12. Apply IRAC (Issue, Rule, Analysis, Conclusion): Use the IRAC method to structure your essay responses for clear and logical analysis.

13. Adapt to Different Subjects: Tailor your approach to practice exams based on the specific requirements of each subject.

14. Manage Time Effectively: Practice time management during practice exams to ensure you allocate sufficient time to each question.

15. Use Feedback Constructively: Use feedback from professors or study partners to make necessary adjustments to your exam strategies and study approach.

16. Stay Calm and Confident: Maintain a positive mindset during practice exams and mock sessions to build your confidence for the actual exams.

Remember that practice exams and mock sessions are opportunities to fine-tune your exam-taking skills and identify areas for improvement. Be open to learning from your mistakes and continuously refining your exam preparation strategies. With consistent practice and dedication, you can approach law school exams with greater confidence and achieve better results.

Tips for handling exam day stress

Handling exam day stress is essential for performing your best during law school exams. Here are some tips to help you manage exam day stress:

1. Prepare in Advance: Start your exam preparation early and have a well-structured study plan. Being well-prepared will boost your confidence on exam day.
2. Get a Good Night's Sleep: Ensure you get enough rest the night before the exam. A well-rested mind performs better under stress.
3. Eat a Balanced Breakfast: Have a healthy breakfast on exam day to fuel your brain and maintain energy levels.
4. Arrive Early: Arrive at the exam venue early to avoid rushing and to familiarize yourself with the surroundings.
5. Take Deep Breaths: If you feel anxious, practice deep breathing techniques to calm your nerves.
6. Positive Self-Talk: Replace negative thoughts with positive affirmations to boost your confidence.
7. Focus on Your Strengths: Trust in your preparation and focus on the subjects you feel most confident about first.
8. Read Instructions Carefully: Take the time to read the exam instructions thoroughly to avoid mistakes.
9. Time Management: Budget your time wisely during the exam to ensure you have enough time for each question.
10. Skip Difficult Questions: If you encounter a challenging question, move on to the next one and return to it later if you have time.
11. Stay Hydrated: Drink water during the exam to stay

hydrated and maintain concentration.

12. Avoid Comparisons: Avoid discussing the exam with classmates immediately after the test, as it may add unnecessary stress.

13. Take Short Breaks: If allowed, take short breaks during the exam to clear your mind and refocus.

14. Use Relaxation Techniques: Practice relaxation techniques, such as visualization or progressive muscle relaxation, during the exam to stay calm.

15. Stay Positive: Maintain a positive attitude and believe in your abilities to handle the exam challenges.

16. Keep Perspective: Remember that one exam does not define your entire law school experience.

17. Avoid Cramming: Avoid last-minute cramming, as it can increase stress and reduce retention.

18. Use Your Resources: If you encounter difficulties during the exam, utilize your outlines, notes, or memory aids to assist your answers.

19. Stay Focused: Concentrate on the task at hand and avoid distractions during the exam.

20. Reward Yourself: Plan a small reward or treat for yourself after the exam to celebrate your hard work.

Remember that some level of stress is normal during exams, and it can even be a motivator. However, excessive stress can hinder performance. By implementing these tips, you can manage exam day stress effectively and perform at your best during law school exams.

Navigating Challenges

Navigating challenges is an inherent part of law school and legal practice. As a law student or legal professional, you will face various obstacles and difficulties that require effective problem-solving and resilience. Here are some common challenges and strategies to navigate them:

1. Heavy Workload: Law school and legal practice demand a substantial workload. Prioritize tasks, manage time effectively, and break tasks into smaller, manageable chunks to stay organized and on track.
2. Time Management: Balancing academic commitments, work, personal life, and extracurricular activities can be challenging. Create a schedule or use time management techniques to allocate time for each aspect of your life.
3. Stress and Pressure: Law school and legal practice can be stressful. Practice stress reduction techniques, such as mindfulness, exercise, or seeking support from friends and family.
4. Socratic Method and Cold Calls: The Socratic method used in law school classes can be intimidating. Prepare for class discussions, actively participate, and view it as an opportunity to improve your analytical skills.
5. Competitiveness: Law school can be competitive, but remember that collaboration and support from peers can also be valuable. Foster a collaborative environment and focus on your personal growth rather than constant comparison.
6. Legal Research and Writing: Legal research and writing can be complex and time-consuming. Practice regularly,

seek feedback from professors, and utilize legal research tools effectively.

7. Imposter Syndrome: Feeling inadequate or doubting your abilities is common in law school or as a new legal professional. Recognize your achievements and remind yourself that it's normal to have uncertainties.

8. Work-Life Balance: Legal professionals often struggle to maintain work-life balance. Set boundaries, prioritize self-care, and allocate time for activities outside of work.

9. Networking and Building Connections: Networking can be daunting, but it is essential for career advancement. Attend networking events, join professional organizations, and use online platforms to connect with peers and legal professionals.

10. Burnout: Prolonged stress and overworking can lead to burnout. Recognize the signs of burnout and take breaks when needed. Seek professional help if necessary.

11. Dealing with Difficult Clients or Adversaries: Legal practice may involve challenging interactions with clients or opposing counsel. Remain professional, respectful, and focused on your client's best interests.

12. Feedback and Criticism: Accept feedback from professors or supervisors as opportunities for growth and improvement. Be receptive to constructive criticism and use it to enhance your skills.

13. Legal Job Market: The legal job market can be competitive. Utilize career services, internships, and networking opportunities to increase your chances of finding a suitable position.

14. Ethical Dilemmas: Legal professionals may encounter ethical dilemmas. Seek guidance from experienced colleagues or consult legal ethics resources.

15. Continuous Learning: The legal field is dynamic, requiring ongoing learning and adapting to changes. Embrace lifelong learning and stay updated on legal developments.

Remember that challenges are an inherent part of growth and development in law school and the legal profession. Embrace these challenges as opportunities to learn, develop resilience, and become a skilled and compassionate legal professional. Seek support when needed, and maintain a positive attitude to navigate challenges effectively.

Dealing with imposter syndrome and self-doubt

Dealing with imposter syndrome and self-doubt is essential for personal growth and success in law school and the legal profession. Here are some strategies to cope with imposter syndrome and build confidence:

1. Recognize the Feeling: Acknowledge that imposter syndrome is a common experience, and many high-achieving individuals, including lawyers, face it.
2. Challenge Negative Thoughts: Identify and challenge negative thoughts and self-doubt. Replace them with positive affirmations and realistic perspectives.
3. Celebrate Achievements: Celebrate your successes, both big and small. Keep a record of your accomplishments to remind yourself of your capabilities.
4. Seek Support: Talk to friends, family, or mentors about your feelings. Sharing your experience can help you gain perspective and encouragement.
5. Normalize Mistakes: Understand that making mistakes is part of the learning process. View them as opportunities for growth and improvement.
6. Focus on Progress: Rather than comparing yourself to others, focus on your progress and personal growth throughout your law school journey.
7. Avoid Overgeneralization: Don't let one setback define your abilities. View challenges as isolated incidents and not indicative of your overall competence.
8. Seek Feedback: Seek feedback from professors, peers, or

mentors to gain insight into your strengths and areas for improvement.

9. Set Realistic Expectations: Set achievable goals and avoid setting unrealistic expectations for yourself.
10. Embrace the Learning Curve: Recognize that learning and mastering legal concepts take time and effort. Embrace the learning curve.
11. Remind Yourself of Your Skills: Create a list of your skills, experiences, and strengths as a reminder of what you bring to the table.
12. Engage in Positive Self-Talk: Practice positive self-talk and encourage yourself with affirmations when self-doubt arises.
13. Participate in Supportive Communities: Join study groups or legal organizations where you can interact with others who share similar experiences and challenges.
14. Avoid Isolation: Stay connected with classmates and colleagues to avoid feelings of isolation.
15. Focus on Your Passions: Remind yourself why you chose to study law and focus on the aspects of the legal profession that genuinely inspire you.
16. Seek Professional Help: If imposter syndrome significantly affects your well-being or performance, consider seeking support from a counselor or therapist.

Remember that imposter syndrome is a common experience and doesn't reflect your true abilities. Embrace self-compassion and kindness toward yourself. As you progress in law school and your legal career, your confidence and self-assurance are likely to grow. Be patient with yourself, keep learning, and focus on your journey of personal and professional development.

Coping with setbacks and failures

Coping with setbacks and failures is an important skill for personal and professional growth. In law school and the legal profession, setbacks are inevitable, but how you handle them can make a significant difference. Here are some strategies to cope with setbacks and failures:

1. Acknowledge Your Emotions: Allow yourself to feel and process your emotions surrounding the setback. It's normal to feel disappointed, frustrated, or upset.
2. Reframe Failure: View setbacks as learning opportunities rather than permanent failures. Understand that setbacks are part of the journey toward success.
3. Analyze the Situation: Take time to reflect on the factors that led to the setback. Identify areas for improvement and learning.
4. Seek Support: Reach out to friends, family, mentors, or professors for support and encouragement. Talking about your experience can help gain perspective.
5. Practice Self-Compassion: Be kind and understanding to yourself during challenging times. Treat yourself with the same compassion you would offer to a friend facing a setback.
6. Set Realistic Expectations: Reevaluate your goals and set realistic expectations for yourself. Adjusting your goals can help you stay motivated and focused.
7. Learn from Mistakes: Identify the lessons learned from the setback and use them to make informed decisions in the future.

8. Focus on Your Strengths: Remind yourself of your strengths and accomplishments. Recognize that setbacks don't negate your past successes.
9. Refocus on Your Purpose: Reconnect with your reasons for pursuing law school or a legal career. Refocusing on your purpose can reignite your motivation.
10. Take Breaks and Self-Care: Allow yourself time to recharge and engage in self-care activities. Taking breaks can help you come back with a refreshed perspective.
11. Practice Resilience: Develop resilience by bouncing back from setbacks with determination and adaptability.
12. Seek Feedback: If possible, seek feedback from professors or supervisors to understand areas for improvement.
13. Set New Goals: Use setbacks as an opportunity to set new, achievable goals that align with your aspirations.
14. Keep a Growth Mindset: Embrace a growth mindset that focuses on continuous learning and improvement.
15. Avoid Comparison: Avoid comparing yourself to others. Each individual's journey is unique, and everyone faces challenges along the way.
16. Visualize Success: Visualize yourself overcoming challenges and achieving your goals. Visualization can boost confidence and motivation.
17. Learn from Others: Read about successful individuals who have faced setbacks and learn from their experiences.
18. Stay Persistent: Stay committed to your goals and persevere through challenging times.

Remember that setbacks are a natural part of any journey, including your legal education and career. How you respond to setbacks can shape your growth and future success. Embrace setbacks as opportunities to learn, adapt, and become a more resilient legal professional. Stay positive, keep learning, and use setbacks as stepping stones toward achieving your aspirations.

Seeking academic and emotional support

Seeking academic and emotional support is crucial for your well-being and success in law school and the legal profession. Here are some ways to find the support you need:

1. Academic Support:
   - Reach out to Professors: Don't hesitate to ask questions and seek clarification on course material. Professors are usually open to helping students outside of class.
   - Join Study Groups: Form or join study groups with classmates to discuss course materials, share insights, and support each other's learning.
   - Utilize Academic Resources: Take advantage of academic support services offered by the law school, such as tutoring, academic advising, or writing centers.
   - Attend Office Hours: Attend professors' office hours to discuss coursework, seek feedback, and gain a deeper understanding of the subjects.
2. Emotional Support:
   - Talk to Friends and Family: Share your feelings and experiences with trusted friends and family members who can provide emotional support.
   - Seek Peer Support: Connect with fellow law students who may be going through similar challenges. Sharing experiences can foster a

sense of camaraderie.

- Find a Mentor: Seek guidance from upper-class students or legal professionals who can offer advice and share their experiences.
- Access Counseling Services: Many law schools offer counseling or mental health services for students to address emotional well-being.
- Join Student Organizations: Participate in student organizations that align with your interests and passions. It can provide a supportive community.

3. Balance and Self-Care:

- Prioritize Self-Care: Make time for activities that bring you joy and relaxation, such as exercise, hobbies, or spending time with loved ones.
- Maintain Work-Life Balance: Avoid overloading yourself with academic commitments. Allocate time for both academic pursuits and personal life.
- Set Boundaries: Learn to say no when necessary and prioritize your well-being.

4. Seek Professional Help:

- If you find yourself struggling with academic or emotional challenges that impact your overall well-being and performance, consider seeking professional help from counselors, therapists, or advisors.

5. Online Resources:

- Take advantage of online resources that provide tips and advice for law students, such as blogs, forums, and webinars.

Remember that seeking support is a sign of strength, not weakness. Law school can be demanding, and having a support system can help you navigate challenges more effectively. Don't hesitate to reach out to others for help, and remember that it's okay to ask for support when you need it. Your success and well-being are essential, and seeking support is an important step in maintaining a positive and fulfilling law school experience.

Fostering resilience and growth mindset

Fostering resilience and cultivating a growth mindset are essential attributes for thriving in law school and the legal profession. Here are some strategies to nurture resilience and develop a growth mindset:

1. Embrace Challenges: View challenges and setbacks as opportunities for growth and learning. Embrace the idea that setbacks are a natural part of the learning process.

2. Develop Problem-Solving Skills: Enhance your problem-solving skills by approaching challenges with a positive and solution-oriented mindset.

3. Cultivate a Positive Attitude: Maintain a positive outlook and focus on what you can control. Avoid dwelling on negative thoughts or self-doubt.

4. Learn from Mistakes: Embrace a mindset that mistakes are valuable learning experiences. Reflect on mistakes, identify areas for improvement, and make adjustments.

5. Set Realistic Goals: Set achievable and meaningful goals for yourself. Celebrate progress toward your goals, no matter how small.

6. Seek Feedback: Be open to feedback from professors, mentors, and peers. Use constructive criticism as an opportunity to improve.

7. Practice Self-Compassion: Treat yourself with kindness and understanding during challenging times. Avoid self-criticism and negative self-talk.

8. Cultivate Patience: Recognize that growth and progress take time. Be patient with yourself as you navigate the

challenges of law school.

9. Surround Yourself with Support: Build a support network of friends, family, mentors, and fellow students who can provide encouragement and understanding.

10. Engage in Self-Reflection: Take time to reflect on your experiences, strengths, and areas for development. Regular self-reflection can foster self-awareness.

11. Stay Resilient in the Face of Adversity: Develop coping strategies to handle stress and difficult situations. Practice self-care to maintain resilience.

12. Avoid Comparison: Refrain from comparing yourself to others. Focus on your own progress and growth.

13. Embrace Continuous Learning: View every experience as an opportunity to learn and improve. Stay curious and embrace lifelong learning.

14. Celebrate Your Successes: Acknowledge and celebrate your achievements, no matter how small they may seem.

15. Focus on Effort and Process: Shift your focus from outcomes to the effort and process you put into your work. Emphasize the journey rather than just the destination.

16. Visualize Success: Visualize yourself overcoming challenges and achieving your goals. Visualization can boost confidence and motivation.

17. Keep a Gratitude Journal: Practice gratitude by keeping a journal of things you are thankful for. Cultivating gratitude can enhance well-being and resilience.

By fostering resilience and adopting a growth mindset, you can navigate the challenges of law school and the legal profession with a positive and proactive attitude. These qualities will not only help you succeed academically but also contribute to your overall well-being and personal development. Remember that resilience and growth mindset are skills that can be cultivated and strengthened over time with practice and self-awareness.

Legal Ethics and Professionalism

Legal ethics and professionalism are fundamental principles that guide the conduct of lawyers and legal professionals. Upholding ethical standards is essential for maintaining the integrity of the legal profession and ensuring the trust of clients and the public. Here are some key aspects of legal ethics and professionalism:

1. Client Confidentiality: Lawyers have a duty to maintain the confidentiality of client information, ensuring that sensitive information is not disclosed without the client's consent, except in certain limited circumstances.

2. Conflict of Interest: Lawyers must avoid conflicts of interest that could compromise their ability to represent clients objectively and diligently. If a conflict arises, lawyers should disclose it to the affected parties and seek informed consent or withdraw from representation if necessary.

3. Competence: Lawyers have a duty to provide competent legal representation to their clients. This includes staying informed about developments in the law, legal research, and being diligent in handling clients' cases.

4. Candor and Honesty: Lawyers must be honest and candid in their dealings with clients, the court, and other parties. They should not make false statements or misrepresent facts.

5. Professionalism and Courtesy: Lawyers are expected to conduct themselves with professionalism, courtesy, and respect towards clients, colleagues, judges, and the court.

6. Avoiding Unauthorized Practice of Law: Lawyers should not engage in the unauthorized practice of law, which involves providing legal advice or services without proper licensure.
7. Billing Practices: Lawyers must be transparent and fair in their billing practices, providing clients with clear and accurate billing statements.
8. Pro Bono Service: Many legal codes encourage lawyers to provide pro bono legal services to individuals who cannot afford legal representation.
9. Zealous Advocacy: Lawyers have a duty to zealously advocate for their clients within the bounds of the law and ethical rules.
10. Duty of Loyalty: Lawyers owe a duty of loyalty to their clients and must act in their clients' best interests.
11. Professional Development: Lawyers should engage in ongoing professional development to stay informed about legal developments and improve their skills.
12. Reporting Misconduct: Lawyers have an obligation to report ethical violations and misconduct by other lawyers when necessary.

Adhering to these ethical principles is crucial for maintaining public trust in the legal profession and upholding the rule of law. Legal ethics and professionalism are central to the practice of law and guide lawyers in their responsibilities to their clients, the legal system, and society as a whole. Continuous adherence to these principles helps foster a just and ethical legal system that serves the needs of the community.

Understanding the importance of legal ethics

Legal ethics play a vital role in the legal profession and are essential for upholding the integrity and credibility of the legal system. Here are some reasons why legal ethics are of utmost importance:

1. Protecting Client Rights: Legal ethics ensure that lawyers prioritize the best interests of their clients and advocate for their rights diligently and ethically.
2. Maintaining Confidentiality: Client-attorney privilege relies on the strict adherence to confidentiality rules, ensuring that clients can share sensitive information with their lawyers without fear of disclosure.
3. Avoiding Conflicts of Interest: Lawyers must avoid conflicts of interest to maintain their objectivity and loyalty to their clients, preventing any compromise in their representation.
4. Upholding the Rule of Law: Adhering to ethical principles promotes a fair and just legal system, where lawyers are committed to following the law and acting ethically.
5. Building Public Trust: Legal ethics contribute to building public trust in the legal profession. When clients and the public have confidence in lawyers' ethical conduct, it enhances the credibility of the legal system.
6. Preserving Professional Reputation: Lawyers with a strong commitment to legal ethics tend to have a positive reputation within the legal community and among clients, leading to better opportunities and client referrals.

7. Avoiding Professional Discipline: Failure to adhere to legal ethics can lead to disciplinary actions, sanctions, or even disbarment, jeopardizing a lawyer's career and credibility.
8. Enhancing Professionalism: Legal ethics foster professionalism by encouraging lawyers to treat clients, colleagues, and the court with respect and courtesy.
9. Encouraging Zealous Advocacy within Ethical Boundaries: Lawyers can be passionate advocates for their clients while maintaining ethical standards, ensuring a fair and balanced legal process.
10. Encouraging Pro Bono and Public Service: Legal ethics often include provisions for pro bono work and public service, encouraging lawyers to give back to the community and help those in need.
11. Guiding Decision-Making: Ethical rules provide a framework for lawyers to make sound decisions when faced with challenging ethical dilemmas.
12. Promoting Accountability: Legal ethics hold lawyers accountable for their actions, helping to ensure that lawyers are responsible and transparent in their conduct.

In summary, legal ethics are of paramount importance in the legal profession. They safeguard the interests of clients, uphold the rule of law, build public trust, and maintain the reputation and professionalism of lawyers. By adhering to ethical principles, lawyers contribute to the fair and equitable administration of justice, fostering a legal system that serves the needs of society.

Professional responsibility in law school and beyond

Professional responsibility in law school and beyond refers to the ethical obligations and standards that legal professionals must uphold throughout their careers. It encompasses a commitment to ethical conduct, honesty, integrity, and a dedication to serving clients and the legal system with competence and diligence. Here's how professional responsibility is relevant in law school and beyond:

In Law School:

1. Academic Integrity: Law students must maintain academic integrity by avoiding plagiarism, unauthorized collaboration, or any form of academic dishonesty in their coursework and exams.
2. Respect for Peers and Faculty: Law students should treat their peers, professors, and staff with respect and professionalism, fostering a positive and supportive learning environment.
3. Preparation and Diligence: Students are expected to be diligent in their studies, adequately prepare for class, and actively participate in discussions.
4. Ethical Dilemmas: Law school may present students with ethical dilemmas in moot court competitions, simulations, or clinic work, allowing them to practice applying ethical principles to real-world situations.

Beyond Law School:

1. Client-Attorney Privilege: Legal professionals must maintain client confidentiality and privilege, protecting sensitive information disclosed during legal representation.
2. Conflict of Interest: Lawyers should avoid conflicts of interest that may compromise their ability to provide unbiased representation.
3. Zealous Advocacy: While advocating for their clients, lawyers should act zealously within the bounds of the law and ethical rules.
4. Honesty and Candor: Lawyers are obligated to be honest and candid in their dealings with clients, the court, and other parties involved in legal matters.
5. Pro Bono and Public Service: Legal professionals have a responsibility to provide pro bono legal services and engage in public service to improve access to justice for underprivileged individuals.
6. Continuing Legal Education: Lawyers should participate in ongoing professional development to stay informed about changes in the law and maintain competence in their practice areas.
7. Upholding the Rule of Law: Legal professionals play a vital role in upholding the rule of law and ensuring justice is served in society.
8. Professionalism and Civility: Lawyers are expected to conduct themselves with professionalism and civility in their interactions with clients, colleagues, and the court.
9. Reporting Ethical Violations: Lawyers have a duty to report unethical behavior or misconduct they become aware of, ensuring accountability within the legal profession.

Professional responsibility is a cornerstone of the legal profession, guiding the conduct of legal practitioners in their relationships with clients, the legal system, and society. Upholding ethical standards and demonstrating professionalism is essential for building trust, maintaining the reputation of the legal profession, and ensuring the fair administration of justice.

Ethics in legal research and writing

Ethics in legal research and writing are of paramount importance for maintaining the integrity and credibility of legal scholarship and advocacy. Ethical considerations in legal research and writing encompass several key aspects:

1. Integrity in Research: Legal researchers must conduct their research with integrity, honesty, and objectivity. They should avoid manipulating data, misrepresenting sources, or cherry-picking information to support a particular argument.

2. Proper Citation and Attribution: Legal writers should provide accurate and complete citations for all sources used in their research. Failing to give proper credit to the original authors may constitute plagiarism.

3. Avoiding Fabrication or Falsification: Legal researchers should not fabricate or falsify data or evidence to support their arguments. This includes creating false authorities, cases, or facts.

4. Dealing with Contrary Authorities: Legal writers have an ethical obligation to acknowledge and address contrary authorities or counterarguments that may weaken their position.

5. Confidentiality and Privilege: Legal researchers must respect client confidentiality and attorney-client privilege when using real case materials or data.

6. Objectivity and Impartiality: Legal researchers and writers should strive to be objective and impartial in their analysis and presentation of legal issues, even if they have personal or professional biases.

7. Honesty in Legal Advocacy: Lawyers should not mislead the court or opposing counsel in their legal writing. They should present legal arguments and evidence honestly and accurately.

8. Thoroughness and Accuracy: Legal writers should be diligent in verifying the accuracy of their research and avoid careless errors that may mislead readers or undermine the credibility of their work.

9. Avoiding Plagiarism: Legal researchers should be vigilant in avoiding plagiarism by properly attributing the ideas, words, and work of others in their writing.

10. Ethical Use of Technology: Legal researchers should use technology responsibly and ethically when conducting research and writing. This includes respecting copyright laws and licensing agreements for digital resources.

11. Respect for Copyright: Legal researchers should obtain appropriate permissions and licenses when using copyrighted materials in their work.

12. Ethical Editing and Review: Editors and reviewers of legal research should maintain confidentiality, fairness, and objectivity in their evaluations.

Ethical conduct in legal research and writing is vital for maintaining the credibility of legal scholarship, ensuring the proper administration of justice, and upholding the legal profession's values. Adhering to ethical principles in these areas fosters trust and confidence in the legal system and contributes to the advancement of legal knowledge and the fair resolution of legal disputes. Legal researchers and writers should always be mindful of their ethical obligations and strive to uphold the highest standards of professional conduct in their work.

Upholding integrity in legal practice

Upholding integrity is one of the foundational principles of legal practice. It involves acting with honesty, ethical behavior, and adherence to professional standards. Upholding integrity is crucial for building trust with clients, colleagues, and the public, and it plays a significant role in the following aspects of legal practice:

1. Client Representation: Lawyers have a duty to act in the best interests of their clients with loyalty, competence, and diligence. Upholding integrity ensures that lawyers prioritize the clients' needs and provide honest and transparent advice.
2. Confidentiality: Lawyers must maintain strict confidentiality regarding client information. Respecting client-attorney privilege is essential to foster trust and encourage clients to be open and honest with their legal counsel.
3. Avoiding Conflicts of Interest: Lawyers should avoid conflicts of interest that could compromise their objectivity and loyalty to their clients. This includes disclosing potential conflicts and obtaining informed consent when necessary.
4. Truthfulness in Court: Upholding integrity means presenting truthful and accurate information to the court. Lawyers have an ethical duty not to mislead the court, opposing parties, or witnesses.
5. Professional Conduct: Lawyers should conduct themselves with professionalism, respect, and civility towards clients, opposing counsel, judges, and court

personnel.

6. Billing Practices: Integrity in billing involves providing clients with transparent and accurate billing statements, charging reasonable fees, and avoiding overbilling.

7. Pro Bono and Public Service: Lawyers are encouraged to provide pro bono legal services to those in need as part of their commitment to public service and access to justice.

8. Avoiding Unethical Practices: Upholding integrity means avoiding unethical practices, such as engaging in fraud, misrepresentation, or other illegal activities.

9. Compliance with Ethical Rules: Lawyers should be well-versed in the ethical rules and guidelines applicable to their jurisdiction and practice areas and adhere to them rigorously.

10. Respecting the Rule of Law: Upholding integrity includes respecting and upholding the rule of law, which is fundamental to a fair and just legal system.

11. Reporting Misconduct: Lawyers have an ethical obligation to report any misconduct or unethical behavior they become aware of, even if it involves another legal professional.

12. Commitment to Professional Development: Upholding integrity involves a commitment to ongoing professional development, staying informed about changes in the law, and continuously improving legal skills.

Upholding integrity in legal practice is essential not only for the individual lawyer but also for the overall reputation and credibility of the legal profession. It is the foundation upon which trust, fairness, and justice are built, and it ensures that legal practitioners fulfill their duty to serve their clients and society with honor and ethical conduct.

Looking Ahead: Preparing for the Next Steps

Preparing for the next steps in legal practice involves continuous growth and development as a legal professional. Here are some key aspects to consider:

1. Specialization: Consider areas of law that align with your interests and strengths. Specializing in a particular practice area can enhance your expertise and marketability as a lawyer.
2. Continuing Legal Education (CLE): Stay updated with developments in the legal field through CLE programs and courses. CLE helps you maintain competence and adapt to changes in the law.
3. Networking: Build and nurture professional relationships with colleagues, mentors, and clients. Networking can lead to referrals, new opportunities, and valuable insights into the legal market.
4. Pro Bono Work: Engage in pro bono work to contribute to the community and gain experience in diverse legal matters.
5. Leadership and Management Skills: As you progress in your career, develop leadership and management skills to effectively lead teams or manage your own law practice.
6. Technological Advancements: Embrace technological advancements in legal research, case management, and client communication to improve efficiency and stay competitive.

7. Client Development: Focus on client satisfaction and communication to build lasting relationships with clients. Satisfied clients are more likely to refer others to your services.
8. Professional Branding: Develop a professional brand that reflects your values, expertise, and unique qualities as a lawyer.
9. Public Speaking and Writing: Hone your public speaking and legal writing skills. Effective communication is crucial in legal practice, whether in court or in written documents.
10. Work-Life Balance: Prioritize work-life balance to maintain overall well-being and prevent burnout. Taking care of your physical and mental health is essential for long-term success.
11. Personal Growth: Engage in personal development to build resilience, adaptability, and emotional intelligence, which are valuable traits in legal practice.
12. Ethical Standards: Continue to uphold high ethical standards and integrity in all aspects of your legal practice.
13. Mentoring and Giving Back: Consider becoming a mentor to law students or junior attorneys, and give back to the legal community through mentorship and community involvement.

By proactively preparing for the next steps in legal practice, you can enhance your career prospects, strengthen your professional reputation, and make a positive impact in the legal profession and the communities you serve. Stay committed to continuous learning, self-improvement, and the highest ethical standards to thrive as a successful and respected legal professional.

Exploring legal internships and externships

Legal internships and externships are valuable opportunities for law students and aspiring lawyers to gain practical experience and exposure to the legal profession. Here's a closer look at both:

1. Legal Internships:
   - Internships are typically short-term, supervised positions that law students undertake during their summer breaks or academic terms.
   - They can be with law firms, government agencies, non-profit organizations, corporate legal departments, or public interest organizations.
   - Interns assist attorneys with legal research, drafting documents, client interviews, and court appearances under the guidance of experienced lawyers.
   - Internships offer hands-on experience and a chance to apply legal knowledge learned in the classroom to real-world cases and issues.
   - Networking opportunities during internships can lead to potential job offers or valuable references for future employment.
2. Legal Externships:
   - Externships are similar to internships but are often part of the law school curriculum and for academic credit.
   - Externships may be full-time or part-time and may last for a semester or an entire academic year.
   - They provide students with the opportunity to work with judges, government agencies, or non-profit legal organizations.
   - Externs engage in legal work, observe court

proceedings, and gain insight into the day-to-day responsibilities of legal professionals.

· Externships may have specific academic requirements, such as keeping a journal or writing a reflection paper on their experiences.

Benefits of Legal Internships and Externships:

1. Practical Experience: Internships and externships offer practical experience, allowing students to apply legal theory to real-world situations.
2. Skill Development: Students develop legal research, writing, and advocacy skills through hands-on work.
3. Networking: Building relationships with legal professionals can open doors for future job opportunities.
4. Exposure to Different Practice Areas: Internships and externships provide exposure to various areas of law, helping students identify their interests and strengths.
5. Academic Credit: Some externships can earn academic credit, contributing to law school requirements.
6. Resume Enhancement: Having legal experience on a resume can make a candidate more competitive in the job market.
7. Mentorship: Students often receive mentorship from experienced attorneys, guiding their professional development.

It is essential to research and apply early for legal internships and externships, as these opportunities are often competitive. Seek guidance from law school career services or faculty advisors to identify suitable placements and make the most of these valuable experiences. Whether through internships or externships, these practical experiences contribute significantly to a well-rounded legal education and preparation for a successful legal career.

Mapping out your legal career path

Mapping out your legal career path is a strategic process that involves setting clear goals, acquiring relevant experiences, and making informed decisions. Here are steps to help you create a roadmap for your legal career:

1. Self-Assessment: Reflect on your interests, strengths, and values to identify areas of law that align with your passions and goals.
2. Research: Explore various legal practice areas and career paths, considering factors such as job prospects, work-life balance, and earning potential.
3. Networking: Build a professional network by attending events, joining legal associations, and connecting with mentors in your desired field of law.
4. Internships and Externships: Seek internships or externships in different practice areas to gain exposure and determine your areas of interest.
5. Law School Courses: Choose elective courses that align with your career goals and provide specialized knowledge in your chosen field.
6. Mentoring: Seek guidance from experienced attorneys or professors who can offer insights and advice about career opportunities.
7. Bar Exam Preparation: Plan and prepare for the bar exam well in advance to ensure a smooth transition to legal practice.
8. Early Career: Begin your legal career in a practice area or setting that aligns with your long-term goals.
9. Continuing Education: Engage in continuous learning

and professional development to stay updated with legal trends and changes.

10. Career Progression: As you gain experience, evaluate your progress, set new goals, and consider advancement opportunities.

11. Specialization: Decide whether specialization is right for you and pursue advanced certifications or degrees if applicable.

12. Work-Life Balance: Strive to maintain a healthy work-life balance to avoid burnout and sustain a successful legal career.

13. Adaptability: Stay flexible and open to new opportunities that may arise throughout your legal career.

14. Long-Term Goals: Set long-term career goals and regularly review and adjust your career path to align with these objectives.

15. Seek Feedback: Solicit feedback from colleagues, supervisors, and mentors to continuously improve your legal skills and performance.

Remember that a legal career is a journey, and it may evolve over time. Stay proactive, be adaptable, and take advantage of opportunities to shape your path towards a fulfilling and successful legal career. Regularly revisit and revise your career plan as needed, and remain committed to ongoing growth and development as a legal professional.

Exploring specialty areas of law

Specialty areas of law offer lawyers the opportunity to focus on specific legal practice areas that align with their interests and expertise. Here are some common specialty areas of law:

1. Corporate Law: Involves legal matters related to corporations, such as mergers and acquisitions, corporate governance, and contract negotiations.
2. Criminal Law: Deals with legal issues related to criminal offenses, representing defendants or prosecuting cases on behalf of the government.
3. Family Law: Involves matters related to family relationships, such as divorce, child custody, adoption, and domestic violence.
4. Intellectual Property Law: Focuses on protecting and enforcing intellectual property rights, including patents, trademarks, copyrights, and trade secrets.
5. Environmental Law: Addresses legal issues concerning environmental regulations, conservation, and sustainability.
6. Employment Law: Deals with matters related to employment, such as workplace discrimination, wrongful termination, and labor disputes.
7. Immigration Law: Focuses on matters related to immigration and naturalization, representing clients seeking visas, citizenship, or asylum.
8. Real Estate Law: Involves legal issues concerning property transactions, zoning regulations, and landlord-tenant disputes.
9. Tax Law: Deals with legal matters related to taxation,

including tax planning, tax disputes, and compliance.

10. Personal Injury Law: Focuses on representing individuals who have been injured due to the negligence of others, seeking compensation for damages.

11. Health Law: Addresses legal issues related to healthcare, including medical malpractice, patient rights, and healthcare regulations.

12. International Law: Involves legal matters that cross borders, such as international trade, treaties, and diplomatic relations.

13. Entertainment Law: Focuses on legal issues in the entertainment industry, including contract negotiations, intellectual property rights, and licensing.

14. Civil Rights Law: Deals with matters related to protecting and enforcing civil rights, such as cases involving discrimination or constitutional violations.

15. Sports Law: Involves legal matters in the sports industry, including contract negotiations, intellectual property rights, and athlete representation.

These are just a few examples of specialty areas of law. Within each specialty, there may be further sub-specializations and niche areas. It is essential for aspiring lawyers to explore various practice areas through internships, externships, and coursework to determine the area that best aligns with their interests and career goals. Specializing in a particular area can help lawyers become experts in their field and provide tailored legal services to clients with specific legal needs.

Setting long-term goals for your legal journey

Setting long-term goals is crucial for charting a successful legal journey and achieving personal and professional fulfillment. Here are steps to help you set meaningful and achievable long-term goals:

1. Self-Reflection: Reflect on your values, passions, and strengths to identify what truly matters to you in your legal career.
2. Vision: Envision your ideal legal career and what you hope to achieve over the long term.
3. Specificity: Make your goals specific, measurable, achievable, relevant, and time-bound (SMART). For example, instead of a vague goal like "become a successful lawyer," set a specific goal such as "become a partner at a reputable law firm within ten years."
4. Breakdown: Break down your long-term goals into smaller, actionable steps that you can take in the short term to move closer to your long-term objectives.
5. Prioritization: Determine which long-term goals are most important to you and prioritize them based on your values and interests.
6. Flexibility: Remain open to adjustments and changes in your goals as you gain new experiences and insights throughout your legal journey.
7. Accountability: Share your long-term goals with a mentor, colleague, or friend who can provide support and hold you accountable.

8. Continuous Learning: Plan for continuous learning and professional development to stay relevant and adapt to changes in the legal field.

9. Networking: Build a strong professional network to create opportunities and connections that can help you achieve your long-term goals.

10. Work-Life Balance: Consider how your long-term goals align with your overall life goals and strive for a healthy work-life balance.

11. Celebrate Milestones: Celebrate your achievements and milestones along the way to stay motivated and maintain a positive mindset.

12. Review and Adjust: Regularly review your long-term goals and assess your progress. Be prepared to adjust your goals as necessary based on changing circumstances or new insights.

13. Well-Being: Consider the impact of your long-term goals on your well-being and mental health. Make sure your goals align with your overall well-being and happiness.

Remember that setting long-term goals is not a rigid process, and it's okay to refine your goals as you gain more clarity and experience. Embrace the journey of achieving your long-term goals, and be open to learning, growth, and new opportunities that come your way. With determination, strategic planning, and a clear vision, you can pave the way for a fulfilling and successful legal career.

Reflecting on your One-L journey

As a first-year law student, often referred to as a One-L, reflecting on the journey is an essential part of personal and academic growth. Here are some aspects to consider when reflecting on your One-L journey:

1. Academic Challenges: Reflect on the academic challenges you faced during your first year of law school. Consider the subjects that were most challenging, the study strategies that worked best for you, and areas where you can improve your academic performance.

2. Personal Growth: Take stock of how you've grown as a person during your One-L year. Law school can be intense and demanding, and it's essential to recognize the personal development and resilience you've cultivated along the way.

3. Time Management: Reflect on your time management skills and how you balanced the demands of law school with your personal life. Identify areas where you can improve time management and achieve a healthier work-life balance.

4. Relationships: Consider the relationships you've formed with classmates, professors, and other members of the legal community. Reflect on the value of these connections and how they have influenced your law school experience.

5. Successes and Achievements: Celebrate your successes and achievements during your One-L year. Recognize your hard work and dedication, no matter how big or small the accomplishments may seem.

6. Areas of Interest: Think about the legal subjects or practice areas that sparked your interest during your first year. Consider how these areas align with your long-term career goals.

7. Goals for the Future: Based on your reflections, set new goals for the upcoming years of law school and beyond. These goals can include academic objectives, career aspirations, and personal growth targets.

8. Challenges and Lessons: Reflect on any challenges or setbacks you encountered during your One-L year. Identify the lessons you've learned from these experiences and how you can apply them to future situations.

9. Support System: Consider the support system you have in place, such as family, friends, mentors, or counselors. Recognize the importance of having a support network throughout your legal journey.

10. Self-Care: Evaluate how well you prioritized self-care and well-being during your One-L year. Consider ways to incorporate self-care practices into your daily routine to maintain a healthy and balanced lifestyle.

Remember that reflection is an ongoing process. Regularly take time to reflect on your journey as a law student, making adjustments and setting new goals as you progress through law school and beyond. Embrace the learning experience and continue to grow both personally and professionally on your legal journey.

Embracing the challenges and rewards of law school

Embracing the challenges and rewards of law school is a transformative journey that shapes aspiring lawyers into skilled legal professionals. Here's how to navigate the challenges and savor the rewards:

1. Intellectual Challenge: Embrace the rigorous intellectual challenge that law school presents. The complexities of legal analysis and critical thinking will hone your problem-solving skills and expand your legal knowledge.
2. Time Management: Law school demands effective time management to balance classes, reading assignments, extracurricular activities, and personal life. Embrace time management techniques to stay organized and avoid overwhelming yourself.
3. Legal Research and Writing: Embrace the opportunity to master legal research and writing skills. These foundational skills will serve you throughout your legal career.
4. Socratic Method: Embrace the Socratic method of teaching, where professors engage students in interactive discussions. This fosters analytical thinking and enhances your ability to articulate legal arguments.
5. Collaborative Learning: Embrace collaborative learning with classmates. Study groups and class discussions can deepen your understanding of legal principles and provide diverse perspectives.

6. Bar Exam Preparation: Embrace the preparation for the bar exam. While it's challenging, remember that it's an essential step towards becoming a licensed attorney.

7. Experiential Learning: Embrace experiential learning opportunities, such as internships, externships, and clinics. These experiences provide practical exposure to the legal profession.

8. Mentoring and Networking: Embrace opportunities to connect with legal professionals and mentors who can offer guidance and support throughout your legal journey.

9. Work-Life Balance: Embrace the importance of maintaining a healthy work-life balance. Taking care of your physical and mental well-being will enhance your academic and professional performance.

10. Celebrate Milestones: Embrace and celebrate your achievements, whether big or small. Recognize the progress you make along your law school journey.

11. Overcoming Challenges: Embrace challenges as learning opportunities. Overcoming obstacles will build resilience and prepare you for the demands of a legal career.

12. Lifelong Learning: Embrace the concept of lifelong learning in the legal profession. The law is ever-evolving, and continuous learning is essential for staying current and relevant.

13. Professional Development: Embrace professional development opportunities, such as attending legal conferences and workshops. These activities enrich your legal knowledge and skills.

14. Impactful Work: Embrace the potential to make a positive impact on people's lives through your legal work. Law provides opportunities to advocate for justice and contribute to society.

15. Career Growth: Embrace the prospect of a fulfilling legal career. While law school can be challenging, it paves the

way for a rewarding professional journey.

Embracing the challenges and rewards of law school with determination and a positive attitude will help you thrive in this demanding and rewarding academic environment. Recognize that the journey is both transformative and gratifying, setting the stage for a successful legal career filled with meaningful contributions to the legal profession and society as a whole.

Continuing the pursuit of mastering the art of law practice

Continuing the pursuit of mastering the art of law practice is a lifelong journey that involves continuous learning, growth, and adaptation. Here are some ways to keep progressing in your legal career and further develop your expertise:

1. Lifelong Learning: Commit to continuous learning by attending legal seminars, workshops, and webinars. Stay updated on changes in laws, regulations, and legal trends.

2. Professional Development: Seek opportunities for professional development, such as obtaining certifications or participating in specialized training programs relevant to your practice area.

3. Mentorship: Cultivate relationships with experienced attorneys who can serve as mentors and provide guidance as you navigate your legal career.

4. Networking: Continue building and expanding your professional network by attending legal events, joining bar associations, and engaging with colleagues in your practice area.

5. Pro Bono Work: Engage in pro bono work to give back to the community and gain practical experience in different areas of law.

6. Publication and Research: Write legal articles or participate in legal research projects to demonstrate your expertise and contribute to the legal community.

7. Specialization: Consider specializing in a specific area

of law to become an expert in that field and provide tailored legal services to clients.

8. Leadership Roles: Take on leadership roles within legal organizations or community initiatives to enhance your leadership and management skills.
9. Technological Advancements: Stay abreast of technological advancements in the legal industry and explore how technology can improve your legal practice.
10. Embrace Challenges: Be open to taking on challenging cases or assignments that push you outside your comfort zone and enable you to grow as a legal professional.
11. Reflect and Adapt: Continuously reflect on your experiences and seek areas for improvement. Be adaptable and willing to make changes to enhance your legal practice.
12. Work-Life Balance: Strive for a healthy work-life balance to avoid burnout and maintain overall well-being, which contributes to long-term success.
13. Client Relations: Focus on building strong client relationships based on trust, communication, and transparency.
14. Personal Branding: Develop a strong personal brand as a legal professional to distinguish yourself in the legal marketplace.
15. Emotional Intelligence: Enhance your emotional intelligence to better understand and connect with clients and colleagues.

Remember that mastering the art of law practice is not a destination but an ongoing journey. Embrace the challenges, seek new opportunities for growth, and remain committed to your passion for law. By continuously striving for excellence and adapting to changes in the legal landscape, you can achieve long-term success and make a meaningful impact in the legal profession.

Parting words of encouragement and motivation

As you embark on your journey in law, remember that the pursuit of mastering the art of law practice is a noble and rewarding path. You have chosen a profession that holds the power to impact lives, advocate for justice, and uphold the rule of law.

Throughout your legal career, you will encounter challenges, setbacks, and moments of self-doubt. Embrace these as opportunities for growth and learning. Each obstacle you overcome will make you stronger and more resilient, equipping you to tackle even greater challenges in the future.

Stay true to your passion for the law and the principles that brought you to this profession. Let your sense of integrity, empathy, and dedication guide you in your interactions with clients, colleagues, and the broader legal community.

As you navigate the complexities of law, remember to prioritize self-care and maintain a healthy work-life balance. Your well-being is essential to your success as a legal professional.

Never underestimate the value of continuous learning and personal growth. Embrace opportunities for professional development and seek out mentors who can guide and inspire you on your journey.

Remember that every case you handle, every client you represent, and every legal challenge you overcome contributes to your growth as a legal professional. Embrace the impact you have on the lives of others and the opportunity to be a voice for those who need it most.

Stay committed to ethical conduct and professional responsibility, for they are the cornerstones of a respected and trusted legal practitioner.

Above all, believe in yourself and your abilities. Your journey in law may be filled with both triumphs and tribulations, but with determination, passion, and perseverance, you can achieve greatness in the legal profession.

Embrace the art of law practice with open arms, and let your passion for justice and advocacy drive you forward. Remember that every step you take is an opportunity to leave a positive mark on the world.

May your legal journey be filled with purpose, fulfillment, and the unwavering pursuit of justice. As you venture forth, know that the legal community stands behind you, cheering you on as you make a difference in the lives of others.

Go forth with courage, integrity, and a heart for justice. Your journey in law holds infinite possibilities, and the impact you will have is immeasurable. Best wishes on your remarkable path ahead!